Neville on the Level

Blooming, Arranging, & Living the Florist's Life

Neville MacKay, CAFA, PFCI

ISBN: 978-1-7751746-0-8 (Paperback version)

"Share LOVE through the Beauty of Flowers!"
Neville MacKay, CAFA, PFCI

Arrangements

A Bouquet of Thanks

There are *countless* people I should thank, but mostly I need to thank:

My mum and dad, who taught me the beauty and preciousness of flowers, the value of having a big mouth, and the courage to use both wisely. Thank you for your unconditional love and respect, wisdom and guidance that have made me the strong man I am today.

And to my husband, David, who continually remains my biggest fan, my source of inspiration and my safe place when things get crazy. Thank you, "Percy," for letting me spread my wings and fly!

Thank you to all my friends and family!

Tyler, you big bundle of wonderful, thank you!

Introduction: For You

Happiness is holding flowers in both hands.

— Chinese Proverb

I have been in the floral industry for many years now, and I sometimes think I have done it all, seen it all, and heard it all. Well, I haven't, not by a long shot.

Working in this incredible industry, I have witnessed so many vast improvements, changes, and the complete evolution of floral fashions. I remember when some flowers that we know now as everyday were considered quite special and elite, and still others that aren't being grown at all any more. It is amazing to see the continued power and influence flowers have on our lives, and I am blessed to have the opportunity to work with something as precious as these.

Flowers are food for the soul and celebrate all the beauty in life, which is wonderful. Now, it's the humans who partake in their powers that sometimes lead to an interesting tale or two. There have been so many over the years, and also a lot of tricks and tips I have learned about decorating, design, and dealing with clients.

Writing for several magazines has allowed me to document some of my more memorable stories (not all of them; some definitely are *not* shareable!), and I thought it was time I assemble them together in one book.

I have had so many wonderful opportunities, as well as learning from many mistakes and goings on, and I wanted to share them with you all. This book is for everyone, so whether you're a part of my floral family, a fellow retailer, a speaker, an entrepreneur, or a retired teacher, there's more than one story in this book for you!

So, sit back and have a read. I hope you enjoy my tales from the front lines of the floral industry!

With Love,

Neville

1. Where's *that* From?

When you go to a grocery store, you see where the strawberries or grapes come from, as they are usually clearly labelled. I find it interesting when buying a little box of raspberries in December, for example, to see where these treats originated. As a culture, we're becoming more aware of the sources of what we consume, whether it's something we eat, wear, or slather on our bodies.

Have you ever wondered where our flowers come from, how they grow, and what they've gone through to get to our design benches? Well, as floral folks, we really should do what we can to find the answers to these questions, as consumers are wondering, many using their dollar power to dictate where we source what we sell. We've all had *that* bride who needs to know where every little petal comes from for ethical and environmental reasons, until of course there's a bloom she "needs" and we are to do whatever necessary (*kill* someone if need be!) to get them in for her.

As you know, I travel a bit, so I get to see first-hand where a lot of what we use comes from. Recently, I had the opportunity to attend the Agriflor show in Ecuador and to visit several flower farms! Let me tell you, this experience was enchanting!

First, know Quito, Ecuador, is far away, and Spanish is spoken there

(English also, but at least know how to ask for the bathroom in Spanish; you'll thank me!). Be aware that you're not in your own country and, sadly, there are criminals watching....I know this first-hand as I got mugged while there. (They only hurt my feelings.) Also, this country is made up of volcanoes and mountains, so be aware of the different elevations as they play havoc with your breathing — also experienced first-hand. The food is good and there're lots of choices, so don't pack a jar of peanut butter. This is a diverse and incredible country, full of beauty, culture, history, and, of course, flowers!

Every year, either Ecuador or Colombia hosts a floral expo to showcase what is grown in South America. This year, it was Ecuador's turn. Let me tell you, these folks know how to put on a floral display! At Agriflor, there were many farms represented, all of whom had remarkable displays of their floral offerings. Honestly, to see walls made with thousands of roses or an entire drinks bar made with roses under glass was extraordinary! I've been in this business for hundreds of years, or so it seems, and this was impressive.

I spoke with many growers who were proud to show off what they have. I tell you, there are a few new rose varieties that will knock you over in 2017! I also got to see and chat with Joey, who runs Alexandra Farms, and of course enjoy all those beautiful garden roses they grow! You know how a dog gets when he sees something dead and he wants to roll about in it? Well, that was me at this place! I felt a bit bad for Joey, as he wanted to chat, and I was constantly distracted by the floral beauty around me.

Now, I went to several other farms as well, which was quite the experience too! The coach ride to the farms is filled with scenes of tropical plants leading to cacti and then pine trees as we travelled further up. We saw volcanoes as we crossed the equator — one is snow-capped year-round and has a glacier (the only one on the equator) — and unlimited natural beauty. If you're a little afraid of heights, don't sit in a window seat, just saying. Oh, and I mentioned before about the breathing issues from the altitude. Apparently, there's a "tea" you can drink that helps, but I decided to embrace my shortness of breath as part of the total experience!

One farm processes 75,000 roses *every day*! Yup, every day. That amounts to about 50 million a year, with 3–5 million that are tossed for subpar quality! Imagine that, right? Oh, and I walked through a 7-acre calla farm that made my brain hurt. It's hard to wrap your head around what goes on: from the time they are cut to the time we get them takes often well over a week! Between the miles of roses, acres of callas, and endless rows of alstroemeria and other blooms, I was in floral heaven. (It was like floral porn!)

Look, I would love to tell you all about how some farms cap rose buds to prevent the petals blackening from the sun, or others who are using beneficial insects and such to prevent disease, or the roses I saw that were 8 feet tall and bound for Russia (they must be compensating for something...), or how roses are coloured to make rainbow roses, which was mind-bending by the way. But I would have to write a book. (Wait, turns out I'm doing just that!)

I'm tired and thankful for that Agriflor experience — other than the mugging — and look forward to a trip to Colombia next year (with better security of course!).

2. Flowers Are Magical

Springtime brings with it such excitement and colour, and remains one of my most favourite seasons. We would pick mayflowers in the churchyard, look for lady's slippers, and listen for the first spring peepers to start their annual love songs. Before planting time, my dad would get us to "harvest" wild portulaca and other native greens from the garden for Mum to boil for our supper, which was also a great way to weed the garden too!

I remember picking bouquets of dandelions for my mum as a child. I would present her with these gathered colourful treasures, excited to receive her thanks and praise for such a thoughtful gesture. I can still hear Mum say, "Oh, Neville, these are just beautiful! [Of course, she would say that about every flower I brought her!] These dandelions are too lovely to have in the house, so let's put them out on the picnic table in the front yard." How grand that was, to have the whole world witness our beautiful gifts! Now, we lived in the middle of nowhere out in the country on a dirt road. Only a few cars passed by in a day. I was happy, though, that they *all* got to enjoy the gifts I gave my mum.

As I got older, I still picked flowers for her, but "graduated" into bouquets of lilac, violets, tulips, etc., (though still getting dandies, buttercups, and Queen Anne's lace as well), most of which she immediately thanked me for, proudly displaying them in the house. Curious about the different placements, one day I asked why she never took the dandelions inside. (She kept the goldenrod out as well, come to think of it.) She calmly explained, "Neville, I cannot stand the smell of those flowers, so I couldn't have them in the house, dear." I asked why she didn't tell me this ages ago, and she told me that the love and happiness we both received from these simple unassuming flowers was something to be cherished, and nourished…never discouraged. That, my darlings, is *magical!*

My dad worked at a fire tower in the summer, and although he was a "manly" man who chopped wood and chewed tobacco, he had a real love and respect for nature's beauty. He had a lovely flower garden at the base of the tower, where he grew cosmos. We didn't have them in the garden at home. I recall the times he would come home and wait as Mum opened his big metal lunch box to find it filled with cosmos for her! That, my darlings, was *magical!*

I learned to count because of flowers, and I learned colours too! Before I was of school age, Mum would send me out the back porch to count all the blue and pink morning glories. There are new ones daily, of course. We spoke of this job of mine some years later, and I commented on her going out each day to count them, ensuring my accuracy. My dear mum is a smart lady. She replied, "Ha! Ha! Neville, I not once counted them. I could have another cup of tea by the time you were finished!" That, my darlings, is *magical!*

There are so many magical moments in life. I fear that many people have lost the ability to create, accept, or embrace this magic from the simple things, gestures, and occurrences in a day. I, for one, will always do what I can to entice as many as possible stop and enjoy the magic that a flower offers with no payment required. All a flower wants to do is bloom. *That*, my darlings, is *magical!*

3. Do You Get the "Prom Itch"?

"Here they come! Quick...*hide!*" I know you've all shrieked that at one time or another upon seeing the "flock" (or gaggle) of our brightest and lightest heading in to your shop, phones in hand, hair all "did" and attitudes sharpened ready for a fight. Just talking about it all gives me hives, or "Prom Itch" as I call this seasonal floral affliction.

Now, I know we can't always run and hide, so let's medicate, I mean motivate ourselves so we are best prepared. We have many ways, including meditation, to help get ready for the Big Day, so let's chat about some.

We are the experts these darlings rely on to get the perfect thing for them. As experts, we need to know what's new, what's hot, the latest colours and styles, and the dates of each glorious gala. Call the schools and speak to the student council. You may think of setting up a time to come to the schools, if you've got the nerve that is, and set up a table of samples. You can even offer a deal if they order early. You could make some samples and photograph them for your website, which is the modern thing to do. But you know they've already pinned about 324 for you to look at on their phones.

Talking to the princes and princesses (if they get off their phones long enough) can have its challenges, but none as big as when the Mother comes with them, announcing, (help us all!), "I want something *special* for my little girl!"

Look lady, I want a full head of hair, a 32-inch waist, and a trip to Tahiti. Let's get real, sister! They are all special jewels of our future, and we know it. With careful, well-worded advice and guidance, we can help each of them get the best.

I like to speak to the person who will be wearing the flower if possible. If it's some bashful boy getting a corsage for his date, I try to gracefully remove the Mother so he, too, can have more of an investment in the decision. Have you ever been to a farm and seen a hen with her chicks? Try and separate them...go ahead!

Anyway, I was at an event not too long ago and talked with a lady who reminded me that I did that very thing two years ago, when she hovered over her son as he (yeah, right!) chose flowers for his prom date. I thought for a second I was going to get an earful, but she actually thanked me, much to my shock. All I had wanted to do was to get the kid interested in buying flowers so that perhaps he could actually do so on his own sometime. Kinda like grooming new clients, but also thoughtful partners for someone one day.

The money spent on a prom is obscene sometimes! Remember this, Petals, when you talk flowers as well, and don't let them suddenly be try to barter! They've spent big bucks on a dress, shoes, car, hair, jewellery, protection or whatever else they need, and the floral choices must

12

complement their other attire. I also find that using words like, "dramatic," "classic," and "unique," help to make for a better sale. When no expense is being spared, sell the sizzle!

Here are some fun facts you can use with your clients. Apparently, corsages were once worn on the bodice and consisted of flowers and herbs, usually at weddings, to ward off evil spirits. Victorian ladies carried small bouquets of fragrant flowers (called "tussie-mussies") while gentlemen had a bunch tucked in the top of their walking sticks. When they encountered a naturally "fragrant" person (no Speed Stick in them days!), they could hold the flowers to their noses.

Who wants a boring old corsage anyway, right? And a boutonniere? Please, most can't spell it, let alone pronounce this old-fashioned word. When consulting with your clients, try this: call every piece you suggest "floral jewellery" instead. A lot of younger folks don't want to wear what Grammie wore, but really, who doesn't like a bit of jewellery? This also opens up a big ol' box of opportunity to be creative! Think of an arm band, something on the jacket pocket, or perhaps in the hair? We are even seeing some starting to carry small clusters of flowers like the Victorians did (though not for the same reason!). By using this term, we allow for more options, we can discuss traditional looks, contemporary styles, and unconventional approaches. So, even if they still want a wrist piece with two roses and baby's breath (which is fine), you as the floral expert that you are, are looking in touch and ever so smart.

There are many floral opportunities we can draw upon: graduations, weddings, formals, junior proms, senior proms, oh, and I heard a good one last year, kindergarten prom. My gay nerves can't take it! I asked if the kids were getting coloured ruffles on their Pull-ups for the event. I was in a mood that day, as I laughed till I needed Depends of my own! And, no, I did not get the order.

Nip over to the dress shop on your lunch and have a look at what's going on in your neighbourhood, too. This will give you more ammunition when the onslaught starts! Good luck with this season, and remember how always in fashion informed advice is!

4. Every Day Is a Celebration

Every day there is something we need to celebrate, from the obvious holidays like Mother's Day and Easter to the less conspicuous ones like Friendship Day and National Pizza Day (there *is* a National Pizza Day, on February 9). Let me tell you, if you can think of a reason to pop the cork, there's a day for it!

Over the years, we in the floral industry have had our special big floral days watered down, what with the whole world getting in on selling flowers, from gas stations to hardware stores, every charity using flowers for fundraisers, and, of course, now the sheer number of floral "events" in a year. All this can cause folks to think of alternatives to flowers. I remember all the lilies we got at Easter and poinsettias at Christmas. Not so much anymore, sadly.

So we have had to evolve and grow to meet the demands and challenges of today's fickle, I mean selective, clientele. That's OK, we are surviving for the most part, and I think the industry has grown stronger than ever, along with the quality of products and designs offered. There are things we also must do now to ensure our continued existence, I mean growth! (Darn auto-correct in my mind!)

Isn't Social Media a wonderful thing? Well, it is if you use it to your advantage of course! Look, nearly everyone has a smartphones, so be smart and use them! Take photos of your shop in action and post them on everything! We do videos showing this or that, post photos of lovely new fresh flowers and/or giftware, and share notices for our upcoming events and promotions. We do a lot of our business online, also taking every opportunity to promote that, too.

Every holiday has its own possibilities for promotion. Valentine's Day is a time that you can get away with lots of options, from photos of a little one handing a flower to his/her mum, a picture of someone leaving your shop with a lovely Valentine's bouquet, or close-ups of a couple of your design offerings. One year, I wrote a love letter to my David on a long piece of floral paper and hung in in the window like a scroll. (That was a huge hit!)

For Mother's Day all the staff got photos of our mothers and filled our window with them and flowers, and also posted a series of photos online of our mums too! You can also do a contest online where you get folks to post photos of their mothers for a chance to get a bouquet for her! I also post pictures of my mum and get her to do little videos telling tales of what it was like years ago, stories of holidays for her as a child and things we kids got up to. These have an enormous following!

Have you used Snapseed yet? This is a great app that allows you to edit photos and add text to them, and once you've done that you can print, post, or email them to your heart's content! This has been a glorious thing for me, and I have often taken advantage of its simplicity for promotions! Oh, and if you're too lazy, I mean unable to do all this hard work, have a look at the many downloadable images offered from our friends at Smithers-Oasis or some of the wire services.

Have you offered classes before? No? Why not? Look, this is a great way to not only sell some product, but also teach those in the class how to work with and use the goodies we offer, making them even more apt to buy flowers from you. Look up "list of commemorative days." You'll flip out! (National *Purple* day is March 26; imagine the possibilities!) To be safer, maybe think about a spring "Catch a Tulip!" class when the tulips are in season and show folks how smart you are. We do several a year, offering a discount on everything in the store that night too!

Everyone wants to do a cross-promotion, right? These can only work if the knife cuts both ways, so don't be too quick to offer something when asked, if it will serve to do more good to the offeree and you. I had someone who said it would be great for me to come decorate their jewellery store for Easter with fresh flowers, *and* do a small demo for their guests one night, as it would be so good for *my* business. Yup. In return, she would have my business cards on the counter. What generosity! And the kicker was that this was only an hour's drive from my shop. I don't know what was wrong with me that I didn't jump on that one!

Anyway, I think this year I am going to celebrate National Day of Silence on April 15, Ice Cream Day on July 16, and, my favourite, No Diet Day on April 24! You don't have to send a card, but have a scoop and quietly think of me! Happy Holidays!

5. Comfort Is for Shoes

Isn't is a great feeling to wear your most comfortable shoes? They fit well, aren't too tight, and your poor toes don't want to break free! (The same goes for a lovely pair of sweats. But I digress…) The thing is, you wouldn't always wear those comfy shoes or track pants, especially if you want to make a good impression or have a little more attention paid to you, right? We can all get a little too comfortable, and in the floral industry many seem to travel along doing what we do and spinning our wheels. Well, let's talk about getting out of our comfort zone and bettering ourselves, shall we?

Have you ever listened to an inspirational speaker? Often we leave more charged, ready to conquer the world's worries and inspired to be a better person than before. I remember watching a designer on stage back in the day and thought to myself, "I want to do that!" But for a long time, I thought I would never be able to. Eventually, I remembered what my mum said when I was a child, "Who says you can't, Neville?" So, I began my journey towards becoming a speaker, presenter, and an "entertrainer." (When you are entertained while being trained, you tend to absorb and retain a lot more!)

My earliest experiences as a presenter took place when I was a child in the 4-H club in Shelburne, NS. I had to give a speech, and it was dreadful. But

I did it. From there, I went on to present demonstrations within the community and beyond, which, as a child, was an incredible thing. It's never too late to start, so for those of us who think they are a bit "past it," remember that apples are as sought after as apple blossoms!

I've done presentations across Canada and beyond, and let me tell you, I still get nervous. In fact, sometimes the anticipation is so intense, I'm wound up like a cheap watch! One of my earlier solo gigs was for the African Violet Society (doesn't *that* sound exciting?). I was so scared! I was up there, barely talking (shut up!) and not looking at the crowd of at least twenty-three, when my long-suffering husband, David, calmly and quickly walked up on the stage and behind me said, without stopping, "I'd pick up the pace if I were you, Neville. I think the man in the third row is dead!" Well, I looked up and this old fella was slumped in his chair with big ol' drool coming down! I was sure I had killed him with boredom! Thank goodness David went behind him and kicked his chair, and the old bugger came back to life!

My first TV experience was even worse, Darlings! I have one leg that shakes terribly, and after agreeing to be on this show, and not having slept for days, I arrived to appear on this live broadcast. Not only did my leg shake, but most everything else did, too. The producer kindly offered me a seat to present. When the filming was all done and I was running for the door, that saint of a producer said, "Hey, that was great! Want to come back next month?" I don't know what came over me, but I answered, "Sure! Call me!"

Then I went home to change my pants. The rest is history I suppose.

I've always had a big mouth and more nerve than a sore tooth, which my dad told me would get me in trouble and also take me places. He was right.

Several years ago, I decided it was time I did a couple things just for me, things that would elevate my credibility and boost my confidence. I tested for and was inducted into the Canadian Academy of Floral Art (CAFA). I've had so many people ask what this has done for me. Let me tell you, it gives you more credibility than you'll ever know! I know you're thinking, "I don't do shows, and my customers don't care. Blah, blah…" Yes. They. Do. Everyone wants to talk or work or buy from the top of the pile, whether it's the chef, florist, or Madam, right? I encourage anyone who is even in the least bit interested to contact CAFA or message me. Come on, I dare you to be a better you! This step certainly helped me become one of the Design Directors with Smithers-Oasis (North America), presenting and teaching all over the world.

I also took the steps to get my Professional Floral Communicators - International (PFCI) accreditation shortly after that, which I am *so* happy I did, too! PFCI is a wonderful group of floral speakers and presenters, and many doors have opened for me after achieving this. As you know, I speak all around the world, and now with these proven and internationally recognized accreditations, I feel more appreciated and accepted.

Now, finally, I'm writing a book! (In fact, I have two on the go!) I have wanted to do this for ages. Frankly, I don't know what took so long. Oh, and

"Neville on the Level" has become a blogger, too, and I'm doing more video work than ever! I guess that often the only limitations we have are those we place on ourselves. Look, loads of fun and exciting opportunities are out there, floating all around us, just waiting for someone to grab them.

What's stopping you?

6. Who's Gonna Love My Baby

David and I have never had children, but we have always had a cat or two, so we know the stress of having to find someone who can care for our precious baby while we're off gallivanting about. There are so many idiosyncrasies to remember to point out: do they know Loretta *cannot* have her belly rubbed? They don't know the warning murmur emitting from her soul mere moments before she destroys whatever they are touching her with when she's had enough! *Oh no*, did we tell them she can have only five treats at a time, and that she can go outside only as far as the bird feeder? I don't think I let them know that a purring cat isn't always a happy cat. Oh well, they'll learn…they'll learn all right.

Leaving a pet or dependant behind, especially the first few times, is a lot like leaving your floral shop the first time. It is stressful. I remember the first time I went away for more than a night. I made *so* many arrangements ahead of time, had every petal ordered and then some, and saw that the store was well-stocked with every possible knick and knack we might need. Now, years later, I gleefully chirp, "Text me if you need me!" as I skip off to the car as fast as my fat legs can get me there. Times have certainly changed.

We live in a world of "I'm *always* available," which is both good and bad.

But we still need to plan for the day(s) when we won't be at the store. I try to think of it this way: we all have to be good to go if someone calls in sick unexpectedly, so why not always be ready? I mean, we work in an industry that is filled with last-minute surprises from births to deaths, so we kinda already have to be on our toes, right?

It is, of course, stressful leaving a business that you developed, grew, and ultimately are responsible for. We have to have the best skilled people in position, trained, and ready to step up, which can be a challenge for all of us. We all have strengths and weaknesses, and of course, as managers and owners, we often keep much of the nitty-gritty store stuff to do ourselves. This can be a *big* problem though, if something happens unexpectedly and you have to leave the store. So be prepared.

Because I travel a lot — and am thankful I have the team in place that I do when I go away — I make sure things are ordered and as much is done as can be. But not because I don't think they can handle it, rather because it's the right thing to do. Think of the times you've come to work in the morning to find everything done and good to go for the morning rush, the fridges tidied, orders done, etc. You appreciate it, right? Well, by doing all that can be done before you go away for an extended time is a show of respect and courtesy too.

I hear about everything that goes on in the store while I am away, believe me (sometimes more than one version!), especially now with emails, texts, and

24

the odd photo of some atrocity or another, and I have seen many! (Don't ask me about the time I was going away and came back because I had forgotten something to see the store in darkness an hour before closing.)

I remember, when I was in England, getting a call from a customer who thought it was in my best interest to know that she was just in the store and saw two of my staff eating lunch in the store. Scandalous! I nearly hired a private jet right there and then. Boy, people really do like to "fill you in" when you've been away, right? I have been told so much dirt I could have planted an acreage by now, and for the most part, I let things slide off me like ice cream off a spoon. What's that saying, "Don't pet the sweaty...," *no*, it's, "Don't sweat the petty stuff!" Yeah, that's it. *I think*.

If you have well-trained co-workers, you will have no problem, or not as many as you may think. If you don't, well, I suggest getting one or two core people who start taking a little responsibility for specific "me only" jobs, so that they can see how to do what miracles only you, so far, can do. Ordering flowers and knowing how much and what to order, along with pricing, are trainable and important parts of our business, as well as the obvious like design work, customer service, etc. It's OK to test folks too, much like we do when teaching design skills. I do it all the time, believe me, and much of the time it is more for my own benefit and peace of mind. The next time someone comes to you and asks what to do about some silly thing or another, ask them what *they* think should be done. If they are right, super! And if not, this is a good time to explain a better option. This not only gets co-workers more involved, but it also gets everyone to think on their feet.

Look, certain things float, so remember you'll always be the one getting the credit or the blame, regardless if you're there or not. If you allow those in your employment to grow and show they care — and most do — or you're (un)lucky enough to work with your family, things will go smoothly onward. Well, with the occasional bump or two!

7. Here Comes the Bride

I have been in this industry for quite some time now and have witnessed many extraordinary events when it comes to planning for, executing, and being at a wedding. I've rushed to get a bouquet done *now* because the bride was in labour (no joke!), made bouquets for a naked wedding (no boutonnieres!), and have dealt with some wacky people who should use their wedding budget to get therapy instead. The boob who coined the expression "it takes all kinds" has never dealt with a bride on a rainy wedding day!

Things have changed a lot from when I started consulting weddings, thank goodness. I remember that if a bride was pregnant, had a baby, was (God forbid!) living with someone, had been married before, or was marrying someone of a different race I would be told ahead of time so there would be no "embarrassing" moments. (You know, I *live* for embarrassing moments!) Now, it's pretty much anything and anyone goes! When David and I got married it was a non-issue, whereas twenty years ago it would have been illegal and unheard of.

So too trends change and evolve, and with social media we are trying harder and harder to keep up with the current must-haves. We are seeing a return to a softer, more relaxed look for many weddings that was popular years ago (shabby-chic, but be careful not to make it look shaggy...) as well as the classic white, but be forewarned, there are as many options as there are brides. "Trendy" flowers like anemones and ranunculus (what a pain they can be) along with peonies (*only* when they are out of season, of course) are slowly being replaced with more traditional blooms again, and we are seeing the lowly a gypsophila making a triumphant return as a predominant flower instead of a filler to the main attraction. There are also a lot of wonderful accessories to add to bouquets, from beaded wire to ribbons and buttons even, so keep up with the new trends and looks out there, or brides will go somewhere else!

Many of us have learned to dread weddings, and although there are times I want to run far and fast, I do love the beauty of a well-made bridal bouquet. We've had some lovely ones over the years that included a full cluster of gardenias and hydrangea ($$$$) to a summery mix of field flowers and garden herbs.

Let me tell you about a few of my misadventures with weddings, and perhaps you'll feel a bit better about your own. (Misery loves company!) I did a rather large wedding out West years ago, and the bride (she was in her fifties then, so I believe she has gone back to her home planet by now) was specific, to say the least. I had to incorporate huge ostrich feathers in her bouquet of orchids, and I had to make this at her house so she could watch me. (This may explain why I'm such a bitch now, eh?) I think she plucked the feathers out of that bird's ass herself, if memory serves me. Anyway, I needed sedation after that was done. One highlight was when I saw her cut the fruitcake (she *had* to do it herself) and it poured out the middle because it was raw. I saw sparks come out of her, which amused me.

My darlings, you never know what you'll be blessed with when sitting with a bride. I had to suffer through a bride who breast fed her flower girl during our chat. I had a bride ask me if I thought her fiancé was gay (like a clutch purse!), and I had to listen while a mother explained to me exactly how to make each bouquet.

I can be direct, and to some a bit blunt, but I calls 'em as I sees 'em, and I don't apologize for it. We are hired for our expertise and input, so when we sit with the party to plan things, this is when we offer our pearls of wisdom. Frankly, I spend more time talking people *out* of things than into them. Hearing, "I want...," (Don't you just cringe?) when it's an impossible feat is one of my favourites. I want a full head of hair, but that ain't gonna happen. So let go of that fantasy, and we'll figure out a plan B. I also allow them to say "I've got a problem" three times before I stop them. If you have that many problems, then you should rethink this whole thing maybe! Often I feel like "Man Landers" for these darlings, really I do.

It's important to know about the venues, churches, and flowers that you will use, if possible. Get out and have a look at the churches, halls, and venues in your area so you'll better be able to discuss that ugly radiator they want covered or the dreadful purple carpets that no one will even notice. Knowing

29

what flowers work best, what you are comfortable with, and what are available and when gives you more credibility as well, because don't think these clients haven't done just enough research to be dangerous. You've got to know more than they think they do.

One last piece of advice I tell my brides: "Remember that although your wedding day is an important day indeed, take the time to relax and enjoy the ride up to it, because you may be a bride that day, but the next day you're just a married woman. And, girl, there's nothing special about that!" I'm just keepin' it real...

8. What I've Learned (A Little, Anyway)

I've been in the floral industry longer than many of you reading have been on this planet, and I have had our store now for over twenty years. Honestly, when I started I had hair, and precious few can remember me *ever* having hair! I have had the great fortune of working with and learning from some of the best in our industry, have seen the evolution of our industry, good and bad, and have had many great experiences from it all. There are many things we've all learned in our industry, and although I can't share some things I've learned over the years (your secret's safe with me, Arman!), I can share some stories from the floral front lines!

Not every event is an instant success. Years ago, we decided to have a small in-house floral design demo one day, and planned for great things. We bought lots of food, set up tables of sweets and drinks, and ordered in a load of flowers to show off and display. Well, that day came and so did the tail end of a hurricane. We had five people show up. Needless to say, it was more of an intimate event. We still did the demo and had the puff pastries, and although it was, well, a disaster in our minds, those who came did have a lovely time. The worst thing was I ate everything in sight, out of frustration and terror I think, and all I gained was a dress size! The next time we did this (with *no* pastries) we had a great crowd, and it was a huge success, due in a large part to those five folks telling everyone!

Try new things. That's how I met my husband, David. He used to come to our store and get two red roses and baby's breath for his partner, and each time, I would tell him to "try something different." Well, one day I saw him at a club and found out he was now a single man. So, I said, "You know how I always said you should try something different when you came in the store? Well, I didn't mean the flowers!" (That was over twenty years ago…) On a more floral note, many of us try new products in our store to see how they do. Have patience, as they may not be a shining star right out of the box. We tried protea flowers a hundred years ago, before they were popular, and although we didn't sell many at first, a lot of people came to see these beauties. Now, they are as common as hair on a cat's back.

Knowledge is power. We've learned that the hard way. People can smell bull-crap a mile away, so don't bother pretending to be more than you are. It's OK if you don't know everything, but it's important to find out and get that information to your customer if at all possible. I remember when I was just starting as a designer; I got a call asking for a "heavy duty Cat" arrangement for a funeral. Well, of course I could make that…no problem! I got off the phone having no idea what a heavy duty cat even was! I thought it was like a lion or cheetah, until our very butch driver showed me a photo of one. I was horrified, as I didn't charge nearly enough, and it took hours to try to shape that monster out of foam. (It's a big back-hoe thing for those who still don't know what it is!) Thank goodness today we have the internet, where we can get information at the ready, so the chances of not knowing (for long anyway) are reduced.

When you have a sale, you shouldn't discount your service as well. We've often talked about this in our store; this is the reason I run far and fast after Christmas so I don't have to paint on a smile when I hear, "Can you do a bit better than 60 per cent?" My nerve, the veins on my head popped out just thinking about that! (Don't you just want to tell them to *get out*?) The thing is, we all have stuff, I mean valued treasures, to sell off, and this is a great time when you can make ad-on sales. We got a huge wedding by being sweet to a couple who were buying up all the old vases we had on sale once. I know this isn't always the case, as for the most part whenever there's a sale you get the drag-ins and never-shop-in-your-stores, but you never know, so beware!

Doing even the smallest event can help — a lot! Recently, I was asked if we would do a demo for the ladies at the Salvation Army. I packed up a carful of flowers, and along with Victoria, away we went to do this show. That was an hour to remember indeed. The ladies, many of whom I'm sure hadn't had flowers for years, were thrilled, and the good karma from that event energized both Victoria and me. The next week, we were asked to provide twelve red rose corsages for a senior's tea for those had who hit a milestone one hundred years. Well, we donated the flowers, went to the tea, and while I and the mayor (imagine!) served sandwiches and squares, Victoria played the piano. Again, this was an hour to remember! I was telling a florist in the USA about what we did, and they thought it was nuts, as what sort of business could we possibly get from doing that. Plant the seed, darlings, plant the seed! Get out and do things in your neighbourhood, whether it's floral-related or not. It doesn't always have to be a gift certificate or complimentary centrepiece.

There are loads of new things we've tried in our store over the years, some great, some a lead balloon (never ever ask me about flip-flops...*ever!*), but every day is an experience. The thing is not to get discouraged when something doesn't work as you thought it would, because there's always another opportunity. Now, I'm thinking of a "Bring a Bodybuilder and get a Free Bouquet!" sort of event. I'll let you know how that goes!

9. Mastering the Three-Minute Waltz (in Two Minutes)

My heavens, time is a sneaky old crow at times. All of a sudden she (I guess maybe "he," but I strongly suspect it's a "she") has once again run out on you, leaving a pile of work to get done and no time around to help! It's bad enough when, say at Christmastime, you've got fifteen "special" little arrangements (translation: cheap, yes, I said it) to do for last- minute Marjorie, but they all have to be good to go in half an hour, oh, and don't forget you have other work coming in as well. My nerves, it makes my stomach turn just writing about it.

Always be prepared! Now, is that from the Scouts or did I hear it on an old *Charlie's Angels* show? Wherever I heard it doesn't matter; it really does make sense. We in the floral industry never know when someone will drop dead, pop out a baby, or decide it is time to get that party organized, so we really do have to be ready to roll at a moment's notice. As I started writing this, someone came in and ordered fourteen wrist corsages for right away. (Really though, who forgets to order fourteen wrist corsages?) And didn't Emily Mayes dropped in town for tea, too! Anyway, the corsage-a-rama sounded like a perfect job for Danielle, so of to the gardens we went. (Being the boss sometimes has its perks!)

35

There are many things we can and need to do to be better prepared for any and all floral emergencies, last-minute parties, and holiday pile-ups. Besides having all the stock on hand to look after what you need to do (floral foam, wire, tape, containers, glassware, Tylenol, a swear jar, etc.), which should be no problem if you keep a good inventory, let's talk having a design strategy in place as well.

Knowledge is power, my darlings, so when you get a "quickie" on the phone or in the shop, you can suggest a wonderful design using what you have in stock. One thing we try to do here when on the phone at peak times is to answer calls with the knowledge of what we can get done right away. If it's crazy in the design room, we can suggest a cut bouquet, or if we glance back and see no activity, then let the arrangements begin!

Labour equals money. The more time an arrangement takes to create, the more it will cost you, so by having a series of quick, easy labour, attractive design recipes on hand (or at least in your head) you will spend less time not only at the design table but also taking the orders. One of our favourites here is a selection of assorted seasonal blossoms (which leaves you wide open) clustered and placed in a glass vessel, upgrading it by adding decorative bullion wire as a veiling over it. It's a design that is universal enough for either Tali, Danielle, or Victoria to do, as its simplicity allows each designer to be creative and unique. This can be done for very little money, with little effort, and can be made in a variety of sizes and colours; ready to suit any budget (or fussbudget).

Another look I love to see in the fridge is a collection of smaller arrangements done as hand-tied bouquets in assorted glass vessels. You know as sure as there's poop in a cat that you'll get someone in who really likes *that* little one, but would "rather not have the vase." Ha, now we've fixed 'er! Take it out and wrap it up. Done! We always try to keep a vase or two in the fridge that we can use as an arrangement or as a cut bouquet in a pinch. This look is such a great way to not only have a good selection of ready-to-go pieces on hand, but you can make some at your average prices which can be customized or upgraded to suit orders as they come in. This really helps the designers when they are stressed out trying to fill all those pokey little centrepiece orders you took an hour ago. (It's a dangerous thing to put too much pressure on people who are working with knives...)

A lot of shops pre-green containers as well. Be sure that, if this is something you do, the containers are kept cold and away from all the flowers as well for obvious reasons like bacteria, ethylene, etc. During the Christmas season we like to pre-chop greenery and keep it in bags, so when we need it we can grab a handful and run. This works very well with boxwood and cedar in particular, especially when you know you're going to make a lot of centrepieces. We also prepare containers where possible with floral foam so again when it's time to rumble we are ready.

Here's a final tip for those of you who just need a little push (or a good shaking!). Use the resources out there to get ideas, learn designs and prepare yourself. Have a look at the Oasis Idea Channel on YouTube, see all the great ideas on the *Canadian Florist* magazine's website, and go to design shows in your area. Oh, and prepare your staff! I have some very talented designers here who know the tricks of the trade that will make for a quick ready-set-go arrangement for that "hurry up!" customer. (I call them, among other things, a Great-I-Am!) We'll be better florists, designers, and business people when we better prepare ourselves for what's to come.

10. Ho No, Not Already!

Some special occasions arrive at different dates each year like Easter, Mother's Day, and Hanukkah for example, but we all know the day Christmas arrives on. So why is it that every year we all of a sudden kick into third gear and run like mad hookers on payday to get "things done" for the holidays? It drives me nuts, as we all get caught up in that hysteria and mayhem, for what? One day, when all we as florists want to do is sleep and scrape balsam and glitter off places where glitter and balsam have no business being. Come on, doesn't the thought of a fluffy bed and lots of medication (your choice) sound better than sticking your hand up a dead bird's arse?

Never mind. Away we go, once again adorning our stores with the sights, scents, and sounds of the holiday season. I remember back in the 1800s when I started, we would decorate the store on November 12! Never, ever would we think of putting up any glitter or baubles before Remembrance Day! Nowadays, once the kiddies start school in September, all bets are off, and the first sparkles of frosted twigs arrive in an arrangement; subtly at first. By the time we've fed on turkey and cranberry sauce in October we are glowing in the dark from the glitter all over us! I feel sorry for our colleagues in the USA who celebrate their Thanksgiving in late November. They have Halloween,

39

festive pumpkin and turkey centrepieces, *and* Christmas décor all out for display at the same time! I've done shows in the USA at that time of year, and it's hard on my head. I suggested to one florist he chuck a rabbit in the mix and call it done for the whole year!

There are ways to get the holiday season started earlier without annoying some dear old lady (you *know* her, the one who comes in to your store with a look like she's smelled something bad), so let's chat preparation for the holidays. Giftware can come out earlier of course, as some folks are looking for things they can stuff in a box and mail to the grandchildren in Fort McMurray. Start using a bit of "winter" greenery in your store; stop calling cedar, pine, and fir "holiday" or "Christmas" greens, and you'll be able to use it a lot more. The biggest thing that really makes eyes roll and heads shake is playing holiday music too soon. Why don't you play a rousing version of "Ho Ho Home for the Holidays" in early October just for fun and giggles? Go on…I dare you!

Open houses and charity design shows are wonderful ways to get the holidays started. I do many from the end of October to early December, and they really do get the wallets opened, I mean get people in the holiday spirit! Try having an open house, demonstration of some sort (the classic "let's make a wreath" is *always* a hit) or offer to partner with a charity to create an evening of sparkly and glittery fun! I hear you groaning, "I don't have time for that crap!" and maybe you don't, which is good, I guess. You can still have a few little "Let me show you how to…" presentations in your store at slower times of the day that last for ten fifteen minutes, which don't have to be choreographed to death. We do this all the time here, and it's amazing what will sell when you take the time to show people how to work with it. I've done so many presentations just making bows with that blessed mesh; I almost go straight! Really though, I'm amazed at how many rolls we sell when I flip and swish it about like a big ol' crinoline from a square dance dress! The more of this sort of thing you do, the more you will sell, believe me. Consumers are intrigued by watching a pro at work, and most won't run off to the dollar store to make their own. If they do run off, they probably weren't people who were going to buy from you in the first place, right?

Clean your store. Very well. I get very annoyed when we go to do a display and everything's filthy. I remember once doing some work for a company and was told, "Just put it together and we'll clean up later." (That's what she said when the bed broke!) Soon enough, we'll be so busy that we won't know whether we're bored, screwed, or nailed, and won't have time to do a deep clean among the fallen balls and tinsel, so take the time *now* to do it right. Who hasn't gone to do a display and, upon moving the table, found crap from last year's holiday feature? Not good, my Petals, not good.

Finally, the best ways to be prepared for the onslaught of the holiday rush: stock up on Tylenol, get some Tums for when the squares start arriving, and perhaps reacquaint yourself with elastic waistbands. Have a safe and wonderful holiday season everyone, and I send love and sweet petals to all.

11. Getting Fresh in the Flower Shop

Boy, of all the issues and concerns we in the floral industry run into, freshness is right up there. In fact, I think this is the most important issue we face! (Although some of you would argue that drinking during work hours is more pressing.) We have to keep a good supply of fresh beautiful flowers at all times, and we must be able to move them fast enough to maintain their freshness.

I remember calling a wholesaler one day, looking for flowers I wanted to give away for a charity. I was offered a sweet deal on carnations, until I found out that these little treasures were old enough to vote! *Never* use old product for promotion. *Ever.* You get one chance at a first impression, and if I had given out two hundred stems of six-week-old carnations that would be DRT (dead right there!) in a day or two, well I can just hear the chatter.

We have to do everything we can to make sure we maintain top-quality freshness at all times in our shops. This means having good talks with your suppliers so you know when the flowers arrive, and also know how well they've been treated since leaving their motherland. Beware and be forewarned if your supplier doesn't look after their flowers. Thank goodness here in Canada our suppliers are for the most part super; at least the ones I've worked with are. Don't put up with poor product, whatever you do.

I know sometimes we think we're getting a better deal if we get a lot of flowers in one order, but if you have to store them for a long time, the deal is off, as the freshness is lost. Order more often and perhaps a little less. You may pay a bit more, but you'll be better able to control your inventory and shrinkage (I hate that word!) on many levels.

If we get lots of flowers in at once, I create a sense of urgency with my co-workers, making everyone aware what needs selling right away. If you have lots of gerberas, let's say, they become *the* flower for every occasion. I had a chat one day with my staff about tulips; they were flying out the door, and everything else seemed to sit there. So, I asked that tulips not be mentioned on the phone, rather they suggest other flowers that we needed to move. Simple plan, right? Well, the first call in went like this:

"Good Morning, My Mother's Bloomers. Well, yes, we do have tulips, but Neville said not to mention them and to suggest other flowers we had to get rid of…" I nearly flipped! Any wonder I have no hair?

Another thing to bear in mind is that an empty bucket, or one with only one or two flowers in it, makes everything look picked over and old. Combine these precious odds and ends, use them in bouquets, make an arrangement, whatever, but just don't leave them there! I know you're in a rush and can forget, but listen, if the folks at Tim's can make a new pot of coffee every so many minutes, you can empty a bucket.

Cleanliness is next to godliness…and freshness! Keep those fridges, tools, and buckets clean at all times! I hate cleaning the fridge, so I have someone else do it. Use a good cleaner like DCD (from Floralife and in my opinion is the cure!). We started using DCD here after discovering that it keeps cleaning for up to fifteen days, kills pretty much every germ and bacteria, and isn't caustic like bleach.

I assume if you are in the floral industry you know how to — and the importance of — cleaning your flowers, giving them food, etc., so I won't go into all that. If for some reason you don't know how to treat a particular flower, call your supplier, look it up, or send me a note.

We all need food (apparently I don't need nearly as much as I thought), and flowers are hungry after their trip. You'd be hungry, too, if you were stuffed in a box for days on end! The invention of flower food was a wonderful feat of science, wasn't it? I spoke to a florist recently who said they never use it. I, in a split second, decided that some people are to be pitied, so I calmly regaled them with the benefits of proper floral feeding, rather than beating them to death. Sad, ain't it, that in this day and age we have so-called professionals out there behaving like that! Also, check out "Finishing Touch," as this product will lengthen a flower or plant's shelf life considerably!

Keeping flowers fresh doesn't stop when you send them out the door. Make sure when flowers leave your store they go with food and care instructions, and when folks take them, remind them what to do at home. Tell them to recut the stems, dissolve the food in water, and keep their flowers in a cool place out of the sun. Tell them that their arrangement needs water when they get home. (I say to give it a good drink, and then have one themselves!)

We sometimes say in our shop, "Flower so fresh, they're almost rude!" Get fresh with your clients, I mean your flowers...or both!

12. This Ain't The Price Is Right!

In flower shops all over Canada, yes, all over the world, we hear those dreaded words, "Can I get that a little cheaper?" I know times are tough, belts need to be tightened, and budgets have to be set, but why do florists often seem to get the short end of the stick? My favourite is the bride who has six attendants, a *massive* dress, killer ring, sit-down dinner, limo, the whole works, and when she gets the quote for the flowers, she wants a little "discount" because she can't afford them! Well, my little Peach Blossom, *get rid of an attendant or two*!

Wow that felt good! If only we could say those things out loud and get away with it! (Actually, I have said that very thing, and worse…more than once!) It's difficult sometimes to serve customers who want a lower price point, but there are ways we can approach these folks without being offensive. (Although it's *us* who have been offended!)

When I go to a specialty store like a bakery, butcher, or fish market, I'm not looking for a discount. I'm looking for top-quality goods and service from people who know what they are talking about. I can get advice from the experts, knowing they stand behind what they offer for sale. We who work in flower shops, garden shops, or combos of gifts, flowers, etc., fall into that same specialty category. We don't sell flowers and plants as "lost leaders" or as little impulse purchases. We offer top-quality products with the knowledge and expertise that come with the territory. So, why is it so difficult for our customers to understand that our products sometimes cost more?

Perception is a wonderful thing, and we must make every effort to show off what we have, sell, and know. You get one chance at a first impression, and it is nearly impossible to back-paddle from a crap introduction. I went to a flower shop in the USA last March, as I had heard of them. As I arrived at the store I saw the windows filled with Valentine's Day stuff. I say "stuff" because it was well-picked over, and remember, this was mid-March! I didn't even bother going in. Another shop in another city had poinsettias for sale in *May*. What's wrong, people? It's just as bad to see those precious little plants, no longer flowering, just barely clinging to life, sitting in shops' front windows for all to see. If you can't sell it, get rid of it! Take it home, toss it, give it away. These sorry leftovers are not helping to give a good impression of your store. If you look cheap, then people will expect cheap. There's a notable difference between looking cheap and looking value priced.

Perceived value is imperative in a flower shop. Offering customers the opportunity to get a custom-made piece is very enticing to many, especially when we take the time to ask some questions that will personalize the arrangement. It takes no time to offer a little upgrade to a plant or arrangement, and the consideration may make a big difference to a customer's — and a recipient's — day.

Offering a customer a range of prices is another great way to build confidence and to help put your customer at ease with spending more. When people ask for an arrangement or cuts (unless it's a specific flower or number), try offering three prices. For example, "Of course we can work within your budget, but a lovely cut bouquet could be made for $40, $50, or $60." Very few will go for the cheapest price, as no one wants to look cheap. This also keeps the client thinking they are in control of their spending choices, which is very important. Never ask if they'd like the tax and delivery included. We all know those are extra services.

Listen to what folks are saying when they come in your store or call you. Words like "small," "little something," and "not too big" translate to "I don't want to spend much money." This is a great opportunity to let your client know what you can do for them without breaking the bank. I make a few recommendations after learning the reason for their purchase and then offer the three prices. Don't go right to, "How much do you want to spend?"

We offer service in our stores. I want every customer who comes to our store to know that whether they're spending $200 or $2, they have made the right decision to spend it at our shop! That means creating a positive experience from the start: a friendly hello, nice music playing, colourful displays, etc. Let the customer know before they ever ask for anything that they are going to get top-notch product and service in your store. Give your customers tips and advice about what you sell, design ideas, cost-effective options, and thanks, and they will always opt for you over a cheap alternative.

I guess the most important thing is to smile, be helpful, and if they object to your prices, don't toss them a toonie and tell them to get back on the bus! Oh, and "have a nice day!"

13. Fertilizing the New Crop of Florists

Isn't it wonderful to see so many talented young florists in our country? Being a floral designer is a wonderful thing, and I am so thankful that this has been my life. Having had my store for over twenty years, I have experienced many wonderful opportunities, from doing floral work for royalty (and several queens!), heads of state, and celebrities, to having the opportunity to create designs for many special events like weddings, births, and other life celebrations. I've worked with many talented people from whom I have gained so much experience and knowledge, and I am humbled to think that I have been able to teach and mentor as many as I have. (Many, including some of my staff, weren't even born when we opened our store!)

I started in the professional floral industry many years ago, so long ago in fact, that I remember when alstroemeria was new, and phalaenopsis orchids were never seen other than on a TV show about the rich and famous. I started as a delivery driver, which I totally despised, but I knew it was a way to get my foot in the door of this industry. I also swept floors, washed buckets, cleaned flowers, and scrubbed the fridges (like I still do), and as I did, I watched the designers, asking all the questions I could about where the flowers came from, how they are treated, what can be done with them, and how well they perform.

I was, before long, mentored by a wonderful European designer, who I thought at the time was very strict (to the point of being militant!). At first, she would only allow me to watch and assist, learn how to use a knife, wire and tape, etc. When the time came that I could actually make an arrangement, I had to use the old flowers, and do so on my own time. I was not paid to be a designer (yet), and she didn't want me wasting flowers or money, so I would stay an extra half hour or so after work to learn.

Think about what I just said. If you want to be the best in this industry, don't be "above" doing a little work to get there. I did a show in the USA some time ago and was asked ahead of time if I would like an assistant. Now, I usually get one or two students or new-to-the-industry people to help me prep for a show. I love having this help, as we can spend great one-on-one time, and they can see how much work there is to do. This particular time, however, I was sent a young lady who I could tell immediately was *not* going to get her hands dirty. (And she didn't.) I had to ask several times for her to get off her phone (or her arse). I simply stopped asking her to fill containers, as it was torture to see how disgusted she was doing it. At the end, I wished her well and sent her far, far away. (God help us, I hope she marries rich is all I can say!) At another show, I got to spend time with a great group of students, and I made sure their designs were shown on stage along with mine. This was their first experience at a design show, and for those who have seen my shows, that can be quite an experience indeed!

Like I said, I get to work with a lot of talented young designer wannabes, and I still get a charge when I see the excitement and sense of "new" they experience as they grow in our business. The thing to remember is, when you young designers are working with those closer to their expiry date, ask questions. (It's good for our old brains too!) Really, though, we've been making floral designs for so long, much of what we know is instinctive, forgotten, or we just don't think it's that relevant anymore. Also, there's more to the floral industry than making a pretty centrepiece, so take the time to learn the ins and outs of this incredible business we are in. Please know that you can *always* call me, send an email, tweet, Facebook message if you have any queries about our industry. I love to share what I know about our industry, and sharing knowledge is what we need to keep our industry vital and alive, so don't be shy! (I'm no better than anyone else remember; I just know different things and have had a few more experiences.)

Ask and learn about our history, such as what it was like before floral foam and plastic dishes. (Yes, there was a time!) I know we learn about Hogarth Curves, Victorian, Ikebana, and other design styles, but also take the time to learn about what it was like to work in our industry "back in the day." I remember going to an old florist's place. They had not only a little greenhouse with plumosa fern growing under the benches that they used solely for their rose arrangements but also stored their flowers in an old root cellar, where it was always cool (and creepy). Another place I visited used a horse and buggy at one time to deliver their flowers. Another had a special garden that people could choose flowers from for their arrangements. (How civilized!)

I still take any opportunity I can to spend time with the elders of our community. As I become one of those elderberries, I appreciate ever more the work they have done for our industry. I have been fortunate to work with and watch some incredible senior (some really are!) designers who I have learned so much from over the years. I am so humbled in their presence. Thank you, Bobbi, Ralph, Rene, Hitomi, Kathy, Harvey, Albert, Kevin, Dottie, Bob, Dereck, and the many others who have helped make me the designer I am today.

14. Just Put on a "Happy Face"

Some of us can remember the "Good Old Days," when folks went to a butcher for great meat, a baker for the best breads and pastries, and a florist for the best flowers. Now, a person can pick up a bouquet pretty much everywhere, from a grocery store to a gas station. (I actually saw bunches at a second-hand clothing store. Really?) When I first started out in this glorious industry, we would bring in hundreds of poinsettias for Christmas, dozens and dozens of Easter lilies for the season, and of course thousands of roses for Valentine's Day. Now, many florists bring a lot fewer plants for the holidays, just a selection for the wire orders, some to please dear old Mrs. Crabby-Grouch who wants them for the ladies at the Home, and a few to make a nice display. Although flower shops aren't selling quite as many flowers (well, roses anyway) for Valentine's Day as they used to, things still seem to be holding well for our industry.

The competition for flowers is extraordinary and, some will argue, has been great for our industry. Consumers are able to have access to flowers in many places now, and are having flowers in their homes on a regular basis, not just for the "special moments" in our lives. This availability has made the retail florist evolve and grow to become the go-to place for quality, service, design, and floral knowledge.

David and I got married in October 2011. (It was reported as Halifax's "Royal Wedding.") As you would expect, we did so live on the radio, and with TV cameras and other media coverage as well. People were buzzing everywhere about the food, what we would wear (we looked *hot!*) and of course, the flowers! We are very fortunate to know some of the best people, and were able to have the best cake, meal, photographer, etc. As for the flowers, Amy and the gang at Avon Valley Floral wholesaler looked after them. Here's the thing: *who would dare do flowers for me?* Well, Avon Valley was having classes all that week, so the students attending each made a piece for the tables, with Amy making some of the larger pieces. They were brilliant in that they were all made by florists from around Atlantic Canada, and celebrated diversity and design. (Every piece was different!)

I've said it before: you get one chance at a first impression, and this is what we have to let our customers know (and show them as they walk in or call us). We all remember a fabulous chocolate a lot longer that a cheap chocolate bar, will treat ourselves to a fancy coffee that we'll savour rather than slurp down in a hurry, or brag up beautiful design for a lot longer than a "cheap and cheery" bouquet.

I was asked once, by a rather snotty bit, I mean lady, what the difference is between a retail florist and any other place that sells flowers. I wanted to tell her that she obviously got off her bus at the wrong stop, but I didn't, which was a feat for me! (Some people just have to come in and dump their bad mood on us I think.) Anyway, after mentally gasping at her lack of fashion sense, I thought I would explain things this way: "Dear; if you want to sit home on the sofa in your housecoat and fuzzy slippers and watch TV, then you may chow down on some frozen fish sticks and fries. Now, if you were having company over you would get dressed, set the table, and maybe serve grilled salmon and roasted potatoes. Darling, it's all fish and potatoes. The thing is, I don't sell fish sticks and french fries..." She understood, then went for lunch.

We sell emotion. We sell love and good wishes. We sell comfort and confidence. We sell quality and knowledge. We sell design.

Floral designers have an advantage in that we can make beautiful arrangements for our customers; we can customize pieces for both young and old, work within most budgets, and can create fabulous and unique arrangements that show our creativity and give importance to our stores. We can use floral foam correctly, which is certainly a rare talent outside a retail florist shop. We (have to) put in an effort to develop relationships, showing our customers how important it is to get the best. We don't have to apologize for our prices, as we offer so many added values that are worth the price.

If you go cheap, it looks like you just went cheap, simple as that. We mustn't try to compete with other flower-sellers, but instead try to make our shops the best experience a person can have, be it on the phone or in person.

By upgrading our products, offering a unique twist on an old favourite (like a cool wire treatment), and of course showcasing alternatives to traditional flowers and designs, we will set ourselves apart from the rest. (Remember the young folks coming in are looking for fun and new, not old and boring and not like what their parents got).

Like the song says, "Just Put on a Happy Face," up the dosage if necessary, and look out for a great Valentine's Week!

15. Remembering the Good Old Days

When I was starting out in this industry, I looked to the experience and wisdom of the older, seasoned designers who have "been there and done that" many times before. I now find myself suddenly being *that* person many younger designers look to! Where did the time go?

I remember the excitement of getting in some of the rarer flowers for us all to marvel at (and for *only* the head designers to work with) — alstroemeria, calla lilies, hydrangea — my head would spin! Now these all seem as common as hairs on a cat's back, and most don't get the respect and gratitude they once did.

I have grown and matured over the years, evolving and moving with the times and our industry, from googly eyes on commercial mums and lace collars around carnation bouquets to splitting aspidistra leaves and suspending amaryllis from branches to use a vase. I started in a little town in Nova Scotia handing what change I had in my pocket to the local florist and asking for as many flowers as that bounty would buy. And now I find myself offering a few blossoms to the children to give to their own mothers.

"Don't forget where you came from." That was the advice given to me years ago by a physic woman (I think it was actually a drag-queen, truth be told). Anyway, those words stuck in my brain, and I take them with me wherever I go. When I think of how things were done years ago in our industry, it is amazing how spoiled we all are now. There were times in North America when flowers weren't always available, and all that could be used was either grown locally (there are still many florists with their greenhouses attached to their shops; sadly not in use for the most part) or could keep for a long time, like carnations and gladioli.

For all you "less-seasoned" florists and designers, I want to you take the time to talk to an older florist, see what it was like back in the day for them, what they used, the styles of design, etc. I have spoken with many more mature (old as trees!) designers, and have been amazed at how things have changed for us all. Floral foam, for example, was only invented in the 1950s. Before that florists used chicken wire, ferns, moss, mud, and even clay to hold flowers in place.

I did a show not long ago and a lady in the audience (sweet little thing, about eighteen and full of excitement) wanted to share her revelations with me on using moss and chicken wire to hold flowers in place. I was both impressed and amused, at my recollection of how excited I was when I learned these techniques back in 1867, and also at how pleased with herself she was to think that she was teaching me something new. Bless her heart; she will do well in this industry.

Some of us will remember the Bill Hixson floral books (the ones who still have a memory left after years of inhaling paint and glue fumes). Well, I got a call one day from a wholesaler whose staff had dug up an old copy somewhere. They saw a "glamellia," and they thought the only person old enough (nice) who would know what this beauty was would be me. I had to squash the urge to laugh at them all while I explained that this was not a flower from the past, but a composite blossom made from gladiola petals.

Ask an old(er) designer what a tussie-mussie is (these were popular before deodorant was invented); or where the term "June Bride" came from (it has to do with crops and cleanliness); or why some flowers were used as a form of communication or commerce (check out how people used to "translate" a bouquet that was sent to get the hidden message, or how much tulip bulbs used to be worth). These are things I think as florists we should know, as this is a part of our heritage. There are books, articles, and all sorts of information out there for us to learn about our trade, our industry, our *art*, and it is important for us to know where we came from.

Floral design, like any other art form, has changed a lot over the years, especially with the new technology and all the wonderful inventions and new varieties of flowers. But the origins of what we do are what have defined our industry, as well as many others in this world. We come from a great line of talented and remarkable people, and I am proud to be a part of that legacy. Carry the torch, my Petals, and honour those who have blazed the trails for us all.

16. Expose Yourself

Over the past few months, I've been a designer at floral shows all over North America (A big shout-out to my friends at the shows in Vancouver and Edmonton!), representing Smithers-Oasis. At these events, I get asked many questions, and I find that these are great places to learn about (and from) other florists and people in our industry. Now, although we're all a little different (and I know different!), we all seem to face pretty much the same challenges and concerns wherever I travel. For instance, a common question I answer is how they can get more exposure to the public. Well, my little Petals, sit back and pay attention. I'm going to let you in on what I do to stand out from all the rest. (Or, at least, some of what I do!)

Over the years, I have had the opportunity to be on many television and radio shows, locally, nationally, and internationally, and appear in several magazines and newspapers all over. Some have said how "lucky" I am. Well, I am very fortunate, I agree. But things happen for a reason, and I work hard to get where I want to be.

Here's the thing: you've got to have more nerve than a sore tooth these days! It's those of us who aren't afraid to do what we have to do to get the job done who will get places. I remember the first few times I did a stage presentation as an adult; I was wound up like a three-dollar watch! I had to lift my left leg, as it shook so badly that it made a noise as it hit the floor! (Not to mention making the man-boobs jiggle…don't laugh, Mr. Waters!) I had to have tables that were skirted so I could hide this affliction, but with each passing event, things got easier, and the shaking finally stopped. (Sadly, the jiggle remains.) I also was terrified at the thought of being on television, and the only thing I could do on my first appearance was make a bow for a Christmas tree. Now, I still get the nerves, which is natural, but a lot of it is true excitement as I enjoy it so much! My mum taught me to keep going and to never give up. I remember her little chirp with her delightful British accent, "If at first you don't succeed, try, try again!" I did just that.

There are many things we all can do that cost little or nothing to better expose our businesses to the world. One of my favourites is to just get out there in the in the middle of things and give away flowers. Now, don't freak out. This is a cost-effective way to get the word out directly to the public. I sometimes take a bunch or two of roses and hand them out, as the cost is little compared to, let's say, a newspaper ad, and it gets a sample to the public. I often give a flower to a lady (or man) or a balloon to a child, and they don't forget the gesture. The thing to remember here is not to give away old flowers! I see this way too often in our industry, and it is a dangerous thing to do. Unless you are giving older flowers to a good friend or family, just don't do it. You never know who will see those flowers, not knowing you were just giving oldies away. Do it right and you'll be better for it.

The same goes for charitable donations. I never give cash, opting for either a gift certificate or a lovely permanent piece. In the past, I have offered pieces to events where I know I'll get good exposure. I even send flowers out (when I can) to offer congratulations to new businesses, art galleries, etc., as these goodwill gestures are good for business.

In-house, we have framed photos of our work here and there, as well as photos of people we've done work for. This is a wonderful way to "talk about" your work and accomplishments without actually having to. It adds credibility to and confidence in you and your business. It's amazing how many people watch *Coronation Street* and are excited to see photos of some of the cast in our store.

Are you on Facebook? If not, then get a wiggle in it and do so, *today*! I've garnered some good business from Facebook in the past few months. It's a great way to let all know what we are up to here at work. I post photos of my work as well as videos and links to my YouTube videos, and many people get a chance to check it all out. This is *free*! It costs *nothing*! So, get at it!

Add more to your web page also. On mine I have links to other sites and videos, testimonials from clients, photos, and even a calendar of events (which I need to update). This gets a lot of hits and is a great boon in business. Use your digital camera to do a little video of your work. It costs nothing, and you can reshoot until it is OK. Post it on YouTube, on Facebook, or on your website and show yourself to the world! I have so many videos out there now (check my website for links or be my friend on Facebook!); some were great, some OK, and others not so good (some are awful, it's true!), but I tried!

Don't be afraid, Darlings, to do what you have to do to get out there! I know you all have the ability to take a photo or to give away a flower at the very least. People will remember you and keep you in mind the next time they need flowers.

17. Growing a Florist

When I started in this industry, the thing to do was to get in with an old pro and apprentice with them, which is exactly what I did. I didn't start making arrangements on the first day, week, or even month when I started. I had to do all sorts of awful things first: scrub the floors and coolers, clean buckets, stuff wreath frames with that awful moss that was more dirt, sticks, and rabbit turds than anything, make deliveries, and sweep the floors around the "designers." I cursed those Great-I-Am designers as they sat and had lunch while I cleaned their filthy work areas (they were pigs), but I did learn *how* to clean properly, the importance of it, and most of all that I am not above doing it.

Now, even hundreds of years later, I still do all that stuff, along with everyone else, and I am thankful to be able to. Along the way, all the designers taught me a lot about the floral industry and floral design. Being so close to them (while I cleaned their filth), I was able to ask all sorts of questions, as well as get a close look at the tricks they used and exactly how and why things were done. After work, I got to try my hand at floral design after observing them that day, using the bits and pieces left, and my work was critiqued the next day on what I did right and wrong. I remember the first pieces that were good enough to send out on a delivery. That was such a treat! To think, someone actually paid for an arrangement I made! (I know this is a great place for an off-colour comment, but I'll leave that up to you...)

Now, fast forward to the present, when times are tough: there are fewer design shows offered, and fewer of us are able to spend money on classes for our staff. What's a person to do? It's hard to inspire and encourage staff, keep them motivated, and teach them new ideas, especially if you're feeling the need for all the above as well, but it's not impossible.

Inspiration breeds inspiration, and this really is the best way to grow in our industry. Gather the staff and watch a video online (there are many, some even with yours truly in them!), peruse florist magazines together and talk about the arrangements and articles, and even do a little workshop together. I never stop learning, and am often inspired by the designs Danielle and Victoria do here at work.

Danielle came to our store with experience from other places, and as a young designer was able to show others here how things were done elsewhere. She had some good ideas, some not so good, but *all* were a learning experience. From her knowledge, she was able to start teaching the others here what she knew, which made her better skilled as well. (And it took some pressure off me!)

I still ask a lot of questions after all these years, and I know that when my younger designers have to answer them, they are learning more and more. We

67

often discuss an arrangement that one of us has made, and often will really pick it apart to better understand the *what* and *why* of the piece. I've gone so far as to "intentionally" make a piece that has something wrong with it. (Many of you who have seen me on stage know I do this all the time! *On purpose!*) This is a wonderful way to get a student or trainee to think about floral design and the mechanics involved.

There's nothing wrong with learning the right way to do things from the start. This includes the correct terms, names of plant material, and how to properly look after flowers. I know we can't know everything, but it can be a fun project for designers and other staff to bring a new fact, history lesson, or other tidbit once a week about what it is we use and sell every day. Where do these flowers come from? How does floral foam really work? What's the best treatment for a gerbera? What the heck is a "Split Complimentary"? Why does everyone like Justin Bieber? This is a super way for everyone to learn something new, so invite everyone in your store, designer or not, to play along. This builds teamwork, leads to conversation, and adds self-esteem. (Knowledge is power!)

We have a lovely young lady here that has been with us for several years. She is now in her fourth year of art college. Victoria is so talented and is a sponge when it comes to learning our art, so whenever we can get her to make an arrangement, we do. I really am happy when I see Danielle showing Victoria a technique, or when Victoria or Danielle comes to me to show me a piece they made for an order. I truly feel like a proud parent around those girls, as I often do after teaching a class anywhere. The look on their faces when they have made a beautiful arrangement is a blessing, and is something we more "experienced" florists (aka old farts) need to remember.

Floral design is an art. We as florists need to remember this, to grow like the flowers and plants we sell, and to nurture those around us so they will continue to blossom. Now, it's time I washed some buckets. Doing this keeps me humble, and keeps my hands soft, too!

18. Do You Need a Hug?

David and I just came home from Peggys Cove (we live about five minutes away), deciding we both needed a treat and a bit of a reward after a long week of hair and floral triumphs, tortures and tributes. (If you ever get there, have the warm gingerbread and soft ice cream…you'll lose your mind!) I mean, really, who doesn't deserve a little reward after a job well done? Think about what we as florists go through: not only do we have to deal with all the ups and downs that business may throw at us, but there's the emotional roller coaster our clients are usually on. It's a wonder we aren't all in a recovery program!

I believe it is not only important, but essential, to thank and reward the good work that not only I do, but also that of my co-workers. There are so many ways to do this, and I have done many, so I'll share some. Pay close attention and please try some out, if you haven't already. (You'll have to now, if your staff is reading this!)

I work with great people, both in my store as well as when I work with others across North America. When a good job is done, it needs to be celebrated and rewarded. When I travel, I always take thank you gifts for those I work with, or at the very least, take the time to let them know how thankful

I am. Here at the store, we do all sorts of things, many that aren't costly at all.

Cash is an incredible motivator, and a little can go a long way to let someone know they are appreciated. A handwritten note in a nice card (with some $$$) can mean a lot, especially if it is unexpected. Gift cards, certificates for coffee, or a movie ticket make a lovely treat that is greatly appreciated.

We set goals here at my store in a different way. I will sometimes see who can sell the most, let's say, teddy bears in a week or a day, giving the winner a prize. This not only makes staff work towards a goal, but it can shift merchandise at a time when perhaps it isn't going as quickly as you'd like. Getting everyone to play the game can be a lot of fun, especially if you try to move something that's been hanging around awhile. (It is amazing how great a salesperson one can become when there's a cash prize in the offering!)

Sometimes when I am away, I like to throw a sale. One of the most successful ones is the "Neville's Away!" sale. This gives the staff the opportunity to sell off a lot of older product, and when I get home, I hand out gifts for their efforts. Before travelling, I also leave a little $$ or instructions with Doreen to buy a treat while I'm gone. A run to the coffee shop is a wonderful (and inexpensive!) thought!

Have you ever given flowers to your staff? Now, I don't mean just the ones that are old enough to vote, but I mean lovely flowers? Many people in our industry never get to enjoy fresh flowers, which is sad. In fact, a lot have no idea how long many flowers even last, other than what customers tell them.

71

Give your staff flowers! Give them *nice* ones! This will not only impress them, but will teach them a lot about flowers also. In fact, think of giving them a "free sample" of a candle, soap, whatever...they'll be better salespeople if they know first-hand about what they are selling as well as being thankful to you! Win-win!

I've talked about my staff on TV, radio, the internet, and in magazines, and they love it. Public recognition is an incredible way to show you love them! Think about taking a photo of a design they made and posting in on your website along with a note describing it, or perhaps framing it and proudly displaying it in your window. It's like an upgraded version of "Employee of the Month."

Gosh, I've even made apple pies to bring to work for all! (How gay is that?) I guess the moral of this story is, "*show your appreciation*!" Whatever it is, do something to motivate those who work with you. We live in a world of depressing news, boring television (except *Top Model*, that show rocks!) and hard-to-please customers, so whenever we can show our appreciation, it is a wise thing to do. Now, after all this great writing, I think I'll give myself a foot rub!

19. They Love Us...They Love Us Not

I hear from so many florists about how tired they are at Valentine's Day from all the red roses they have to schlep out. I know, I know, a red rose is *the* symbol of love, *blah, blah, blah*....But give me a break, there are other flowers to choose from, and it is up to us to educate and encourage our customers to try something a little different.

Let me tell you a story. (Forgive me if you've heard it before; it's too good not to share.) Many years ago, there was a lovely young man who would come in my store every other week and buy a red rose and baby's breath. Every time he came in, I would suggest he try something different. Well, this went on for some time until he finally stopped coming in altogether. One night I saw him out at a club, and I asked him why we hadn't seen him in the store, and he replied that he had split with his partner. I said, "You know, every time you got that rose, I suggested you try something different...well, I didn't mean the flower." That corny line landed me a date, and over twenty years ago this March, David and I are happily *not* giving each other a red rose every other week!

Now, I'm not suggesting that you all go *that* far when training educating your customers. But there are ways to change a person's mind.

73

Teaching a customer, especially a young one, isn't that hard, and all it takes is a little coaxing to sway them to try a different flower or colour. Ask them if they've ever tried something different like a calla lily, tulip, or a lovely mix of flowers, to include with a red rose. Suggest an assortment of colours of roses rather than just red, and tell them to make note of the favourite one. This will help them for future gifts, and will make for a loyal customer.

I had a fellow recently come in our store all shaky and excited because he was going to propose to his girlfriend. (I saw the ring...I'd marry him for that rock!) Anyway, he had come in our store the year before to buy flowers for his girlfriend for Valentine's Day, and we suggested he try a more unique approach and not be so predictable. Well, it worked, and the bouquet of callas he gave his lady proved a winner! (Apparently she didn't like roses... something he didn't know before this!)

We sell floral designs in our stores, don't we? Well, this is a great time and opportunity to show off what we can do! Offer your customer as an alternative a stylized vase arrangement (to include roses if necessary) in a lovely vase. This is wonderful, especially if it is going to a workplace like an office, as all eyes will be on it, seeing how thoughtful and unique this gift is. Also if you can, suggest the vase can be used for future bouquets, it may well make for a repeat and loyal customer. You can offer a (little) discount if you want, on the next bouquet when they do this, too.

Another thing we've done for fellows who are not home for Valentine's

Day is to offer sending eleven roses instead of twelve, with a note that they would bring the twelfth personally. We've also been able to set up a monthly floral delivery for a year by simply suggesting it, too.

Valentine's is a day of love, hormones and emotions, and we have to brace ourselves for it all to come flooding in. As busy as we are, it is so important to actually talk to our customers, in order to get an idea of what we can do for them. Sometimes, all it takes is a few simple questions, or a positive reinforcement to make the sale. I mean really, there are so many things to choose from, and at Valentine's Day there are many who are first-time flower buyers, and don't know the exotic beauty of an orchid plant, or the cheerfulness that a vase of tulips can bring.

The thing is, it's up to us to change the world. We have to stop being the, "What would you like to have," and, "How much do you want to spend?" order-takers, and become the, "Let me show you some beautiful choices," and, "For a beautiful bouquet, you should spend…" floral sales people that I know we can, and must be! Train your staff, even those who are "temporary help-to-answer-the-phones," to know that there are options. Keep smiling, even on the phone. (It does make a difference.) And oh, please, stop moaning and groaning out loud about those poor red roses. They *still* are the number one flower choice. Big kiss everyone for a flower-full Valentine's Day!

20. Pass the Fruitcake

I remember when fruitcake was an essential part of the holiday preparations. (I used to help my mum cut up cherries for the cake, what I didn't eat!) And if you didn't get it done early enough, you'd be in trouble! I guess it's the same sort of thing in our flower shops: get things ready before the rush starts. Hurry before you're in a hurry, so to speak. (We live in a crazy world!)

There are many things that we can do to better prepare for the holiday cash grab, I mean celebrations, and with a little planning, life can be a lot easier. We can have open houses, which can be a success provided the weather is good and that you don't forget to invite someone. I remember having one that was a total writeoff because of a storm, which meant we were eating mini quiches for a week! But assuming the weather holds, open houses are a great way to show off your new product, giving your customers a preview of what's to come. Offer samples, prizes, discounts, and demonstrations if possible. You don't have to get too fancy with a demo; one of the most successful ones I had was on making bows of all things!

Get in touch with your local media, charity groups that are having events, and other businesses that may be holding open houses or functions to offer your product for sale, a freebie or sample maybe, a gift certificate, or maybe even offer to come do a demo of some sort. I do several of these at this time of year for charities, and find that it is a great way to show a product that perhaps you are overstocked with.

Really though, the best marketing you can do in your store is actually *in your store!* The holiday season is when we can hang, drape, glitz, and cascade beautiful things throughout the store, and we really must show, where we can, what can be done with all our lovely goodies! For example, we carry sinamay (that wide mesh nylon…you know what I mean), and I make a bow with a whole roll and hang it above the ribbon display. We have to do another one almost daily during the holiday season as someone *needs* to have it. We sell many rolls because of what people see, and especially if they get to actually see us make this miracle called a bow! I guess not everyone has the visionary sense that we all possess, shocking as *that* sounds. Thank goodness for that!

Displays during the holidays can start to look tired very quickly when we start having to pick and pull from them as we need the garland, pick, cone, or whatever, so it is imperative that we keep things fresh and lovely. You know there will always be someone in your store for the first time and you need to make the right impression every time. I remember a person I worked with some years ago that had done quite a pretty display in the window with garlands, ribbons, the whole lot. It was lovely! The thing was though, she had used one-off pieces for the whole thing, so people were coming in for "that ribbon" and "this garland," and we had none for sale. Nothing will frost a

Christmas cookie faster than that, my Petals! Please be sure that whatever you have in the window or in a display you also have in stock to sell or you are willing to take it out of the display for the customer.

In our store, we like to create transitional window displays, as realistically we have little or no time to redo a window in December (the nerves are pretty much rubbed raw by then!). By working with a good base, which includes a lot of lights and greenery, we're able to remove certain features and focuses in the windows, and by the end of it all, when we are getting a lot of people in the store, we start using vases of lovely fresh flowers, which makes for a stunning decadent look that is always well received and remembered.

The whole point is to keep your shop looking fresh and new the entire way through the season. I get tired of a window or other display (including a Christmas tree) that has been sitting there, looking the same on December 19th as it did on November 1st, so your regular customers as well as your co-workers do, too. You'll sell a lot more by moving things around, too, even if it's just the same old poop but just in different piles, as "they" say. (I'd love to meet "they" someday, wouldn't you?)

Now, go get the garlands and baubles priced, out for sale, and ready to shine. And before you get too wired this Christmas, make sure you have lots of Tylenol, water, Band-Aids, and oh, and don't forget the fruitcake! Happy holidays everyone!

21. Mommy Dearest

Do you remember when Mommy was the most important person in the world? Mine still is, although there are a couple of close seconds now as well. To every person buying flowers at Mother's Day, their mom *is* that person, so regardless how busy we are we'd better not forget it! We all have, or had, a mother (although I think some politicians were Satan's spawn), and many are or will be a mother.

Busy at Mother's Day? I guess I am! On top of all the "regular" work there is for the week, I am doing a fitness campaign for the radio (imagine!), a TV spot, and on Mother's Day I'm dressing as a prince (not a queen) to read stories at a tea party for 250 little girls in support of the Children's' Wish Foundation. I will surely be medicated, or at least on therapy by the end of it all! Anyway, here are some of my thoughts on Mother's Day and what can be done to help ease the pain of the chaos. (It works for me anyway!)

I think the thing we all have to do in our industry, especially at holiday times of stress like Mother's Day, is practice empathetic and sympathetic listening. There's nothing worse than having the person you are entrusting an order with act like they could give a crap whether your mother likes roses, has allergies, or can't stand the colour red! (Thank goodness my mother isn't the fussy type — she's thankful for any gift!)

We must let our clients know that although we are very busy, we will put our full attention to their order when we do the work. I know, I know, some of you are griping under your breath as you read this and are thinking, "You must be *nuts*, Neville!" Well, yes, I am, but that's for another story. I will tell you, though, that there are ways we can be good listeners and good salespeople, and yet stay on top of the day at the same time. Developing a good relationship with your client need not take a long time, and by using the right wording, you can make your life a whole lot easier.

Meet your client halfway if you can. By this I mean simply agree with some of what they are telling you, before you grab hold of the sale and keep control: "My mother doesn't like smelly lilies!" can be met with, "I agree, many folks dislike that strong fragrance! What I find has been really popular this season is a colourful mix of unscented flowers and greenery, like gerbera daisies, iris, etc." (Or choose flowers that you want to move quickly!) See, you've made a friend!

I know that many of us hire extra staff to answer the phones at Mother's Day. I have issues with this practice, too, in that often we get first-time buyers during holidays, and they get one chance to receive a first impression — so it had better be a good one! I called a shop recently asking for amaryllis. Not only did the person at the other end not know what I was talking about, but also admitted to not knowing a thing about any of the products, so if I wanted something, she would write it down and let the boss know later. Nice. I guess the simple moral to this story is to train your staff to at least a minimal level, and also to let them know that it's OK to let a client know you are new and as a new staff member, you will find either a more experienced person or would source the information and call back ASAP.

Please do not underestimate your customer's budget! I get a sick feeling in my gut when I hear, "Do you want that to include tax and delivery?" instead of, "And of course there will be tax and delivery on top." Most folks also know that there is tax on everything, so if we ask if they'd like it included, they may say yes. Try offering a client three price ranges for an arrangement, like $50, $75, and $100. Most often they will go for at least the middle if not the higher price. (Really, who wants to look cheap?)

I also see salespeople who can't (or won't) work outside their own pocketbook. I had a young lady work here, years ago, who I heard telling a client to go to the dollar store to get a few stones and a glass, and then they could add a bit of greenery, etc., *blah, blah*, and it wouldn't cost much! I nearly stroked out when I saw she was talking to a multi-millionaire who could have bought the whole store, walls and all, with what fell in the bottom of her purse! (Now you know why I am bald!) There are a lot of things in my store I could never begin to afford for myself, but as a salesperson, I know I can sell them to others.

I try to ask questions when I can to help a client with their choices and decisions. Get the address where Mom lives as that often will tell a tale. Also, without blatantly asking (although I'm OK with that too) ask her age, if she travels, colour likes and dislikes, etc. You can do this with simple conversation, and then once you know a little about the recipient, then you can go for the sale. Don't get too nosy; just get enough information to help you make the sale. I use questions that can guide a person to a certain flower that I need to sell. If I have a lot of roses, I may ask, "Does your mom have a garden or did she have one...really? We've just received a shipment of roses that are fabulous and would make quite a statement on their own!" This not only will make your life easier by selling some of those roses, but it instills a sense of confidence in you from your client and strengthens your credibility. Again, let your client know that you do care about this order (that includes orders from other florists, too) and they will be back for more.

I know we are all crazy at Mother's Day, and patience is thin. It is a perfect time though to generate a larger client base and to develop emotional bonds with your customers. So, this Mother's Day remember to smile, use good eye contact, pay attention, eat good food, and say "thank you"! Have a wonderful and happy Mother's Day everyone! Oh, and rest up...wedding season has started!

22. Prom Flowers, Like Whatever

Like, have you ever listened closely to some people who are, like, under the age of, like, twenty? I try not to, but I did have the opportunity to recently, and I actually counted the number of times she said "like." Seventeen. In the span of a few minutes. (I, like, gagged a little.) Anyway, I really wanted to have a chat with her about trends, but after all that, I decided to watch MuchMusic, read a teen magazine (what an experience *that* was!), and to check things with some florist friends of mine. The things I do for research! (Just you wait till Gay Pride Week!)

I actually did go to my prom many years ago, and although I remember it as a bit of a "confusing" time for me (don't ask!), it was an exciting time as well. Girls then had to have new dresses, shoes, polish and paint; the boys got all dressed up and put on Dad's Aqua Velva and pretend to shave those few little whiskers. Good times, good times! Although times have changed to a big degree, the excitement is still there, and now I believe there is more pressure to look "fantabulous" (another new word I learned) than there ever was when I was that age.

Prom and grad season is a great time for us as florists! *Ha!* Really, it is! I know there will be many "pains" coming in (usually in packs of three to five), all chewing gum and talking at the same time, desperately trying to match perfectly their bubble gum chiffon, or whatever colour they have in tow. Remember, these folks will one day get married, have babies, or buy a home (not necessarily in that order!) and will need flowers. I look at these young folks as an investment, sometimes gritting my teeth with a smile to get through it all, but knowing that if they aren't spooked, they'll be back for more, and hopefully more trusting of our capabilities.

I was talking to Robin at Jean's Flowers in Truro, NS, and she said that we have to remember these youth think the whole universe revolves around getting the perfect dress, hair, polish, and ultimately, flowers, so they think that florists also should be totally engrossed in finding the perfect match.

As florists, we really should be up on all the newest trends out there, whether it's colour, style, or accessories. I find that it doesn't hurt to look at magazines to see the newest looks. Our wholesalers are great resources for new ideas, so ask them, too, what they are getting in that is different and novel.

Here's the scoop: bling equals *cha-ching*! (Liberace had it all figured out even then!) Glitter and glitz is everywhere now, and people of all ages, especially the younger ones (and the really old ladies), are embracing this trend. Also, the words "corsage" and "boutonniere" are a little dated to some people, as this reminds them of their parents. I sometimes talk of "body flowers" to the younger crowd, and that seems more up with the times. Whatever you call them, people are still wearing them and looking to us for advice and guidance.

To many florists, getting enough flowers to make custom corsages for everyone is totally out of the question. Robin told me that in her shop they offer colour matches using a mixture of flowers and shades. For example, a lavender dress could have a corsage made from a mixture of delphinium, statice, and wax flower, glued with greenery. Robin tells me this has been very good for all, and they have no troubles satisfying a wide range of tastes.

Mike from Kelly's Flowers in Summerside, PEI, tells me that he is finding a trend there towards nosegays and little tussie-mussies. He tells me that when a lady has one of these, she is the talk of the night (in a good way!), and that this is also a great alternative to a wrist corsage. Cymbidium orchids are hot too, Mike says. I find they are here, also. Both of us agree that so long as there is a bit of bling, you are good to go! I find, too, that this trend of bling doesn't apply just to the ladies. The men like it too! A little goes a long way on a boutonniere, so be careful not to scare him with too many jewels! (Now if it was for me, bring it on, the more the better!)

There are still traditional people out there who love the roses and baby's breath full meal deal, so don't think you're out of touch by offering this look. Often we see even the trendiest people turn traditional for their own special event, so have a good dialogue with your client. Even if you have to fake it after hours of consultation, try to look interested!

Anyway, do what you know and what you think is best. Listen to what the youth are looking for, and roll with the times. We need to guide and teach these hormone-charged, credit card carrying, "I'm so good" offspring of the X, Y, or Z generation (who knows anymore?). We can't fight progress. Although I have my limits, I know what battles to fight.

So, like, check out the latest rage, modify it to suit, like, needs, and know that this is, like, a good time to gain the confidence of the younger generation! Build a bridge over that gap. Big kiss to all, and have, like, an awesome day!

23. Get Your Party Dress On

I *love* getting ready for a party, don't you? From getting your hair done (if that's an option) to choosing what to wear, planning a night out can be a lot of fun. For the people going to and participating in the event, that is. As a person who so often finds himself on the other side of that door, I can tell you it's quite different from that side. But, I seem to be preaching to the choir, right? You all know what a time we floral designers can have when doing the work for a party, wedding, or other event. So, gather round and I'll tell you a few stories from the front lines and tips on what to do that may make things go more smoothly. I may even offer suggestions on how to get through it all without self-medicating!

I have done flowers for all sorts of events, from backstage flowers for Sir Elton John (the drama, Darling, the drama!), large fussy weddings for spoiled Daddy's Little Princesses, and intimate dinner parties for a stodgy bunch of Great-I-Ams, to one of my favourites, flowers for HRM Queen Elizabeth and HRH Prince Philip! Each event can be unique and hopefully a positive thing, and for us, a profitable endeavour!

When I was asked to work on floral pieces for the royal family, I did what most any florist would do, and once I changed my clothes, I set up a meeting with the people in charge to go over things in detail. Now, there were protocols, security issues, specific rather priceless containers, as well as concerns like scents and colour preferences that all had to be dealt with, so things took a bit of time before we could start arranging flowers. I will say, though, that on the day I went to set up the flowers at their Canadian residence, I was pretty excited. (Yup, I did get to go in Her Majesty's bedroom. And ask me sometime to tell you about how I almost got a selfie on the royal throne in the washroom!)

I try to get to know the people I work with for events also, and I strongly suggest you develop a relationship with all you work with as well. There's nothing so cutting as when we are referred to as "just the florist" by some "just out of trade school with barely a passing grade" party planner! (That was tried on me once, just once. I think she is selling cookies somewhere now.) I remember setting up flowers for a big (*big*) wedding and witnessed the "planner" tear a strip off a young gal who was putting cloths on tables, but apparently not quite fast enough or well enough. I just *had* to go remind that old crow that we all are merely the help, hired to do a job, and without everyone doing their thing, the event wouldn't be a success. Then I went to the girl, who by now was crying and a little shaken, and whispered in her ear, "Never mind, Petal. Remember that she is old and will be dead long before you!" You know, several years later it was true, and I also got to do the flowers for that girl's wedding! Snap!

Watch out for the "send me a sample" people, who want your ideas and suggestions, then turn around and do their own thing. Many of us have been stung; I know I sure have. So I take the time to see who I am dealing with before I offer too much advice. Like my mum told me, "Don't give it away, dear." This is why it's important to develop relationships with those you work with, so if a new one comes along, you'll be able to ask others what the scoop is in advance. In our industry, we are judged on our last event, and if the event is a disaster because of something else and not the flowers, you may well still find your reputation twisted in with all the other crap. (You've heard of being an "A-hole by association"?) I found myself in that very situation years ago, when a coordinator didn't coordinate well at all, sending flowers to the wrong place, as well as the dessert and cake. People remembered the flowers were late and they came from me. Lovely. (I think she's dead now, too…hmmm!)

I love to give advice, offer opinions, and explain ways to make an event a better success, and that is what makes us unique and special in the party world. Take the time to be a guidance counsellor (I like to call myself "Man Landers") for your clients and the folks you work with, and you will gain a lot of respect and credibility.

Another thing to do is to invite yourself to as many venues as possible! It is so important to have a visual of what a space is like, so when you meet with a client you can better make suggestions about placement, colour, etc. It's on par with going to a travel agent who has been to the place you want to go, or to a restaurant and the server has actually eaten what you're thinking of ordering.

Now, go squeeze into that little black number, slap on a little lippie, pour a big glass of your favourite bevy, and watch the last season of *Downton Abbey*. It's *always* a party there!

24. Putting the Fun Back in Funerals

I remember the first time I delivered flowers to a funeral home. The lovely and ever so helpful gentleman there suggested I take the piece directly into the viewing room for placement, and I reluctantly followed him. There was old Mr. So-and-so, lying in his casket, wearing a grey suit and skin to match. The funeral fellow was *so* pleased at his work and how "firm' the old guy was still (I didn't ask how long he'd been laying there) that he told me to touch his cheek. I did not. I found out later that the folks I worked with actually set that all up to see if it would freak me out. I will say I pooped a little but tried my best to remain professional. I think this was the same gang that sent me on a delivery to a hotel for a lady named "Black Magic," who met me at the door wearing a towel around her waist and nothing else, asking me in to get a "tip." That's when I lost the last shred of my heterosexuality.

Funerals are a part of life, and an important part of a florists life for sure! Amid all the sadness that generally accompanies funerals, it is also sad to see that too many of us are still stuck in the past when it comes to funeral design and working with funeral homes. I know the standard casket spray of red, pink, or white roses with a huge bow and maybe even a ribbon across it is pretty much the norm, but there are *so* many more options now than ever. We all need to embrace these choices.

I'm sure you've received a call asking for an arrangement that doesn't look like a "funeral piece"; we all have. More and more we are seeing a custom approach to funeral design, and less of "page 36 in pink," which is refreshing. I've done some unique funeral pieces over the years, from making a spray on a guitar, to a three-foot wide butterfly out of just ivy, to covering a bicycle with flowers. Now, you can buy pre-made foam shapes that make life so much easier. My all-time favourite (*not!*) was a casket spray I made with a nasty old dried up *wasp nest* in the middle of it! I guess this guy was into insects, whereas I am certainly not.

Funeral directors are not usually florist experts, and it's up to us to speak with them now and then, offering suggestions, advice and upgrades as they pertain to our industries. There have been so many advances in floral design, products, containers, and flower choices, but if we don't tell our funeral friends, perhaps they'll never know.

Many of us already have (good or bad) relationships with funeral homes, or at least we are known for what we can (and can't in some cases) do. I've always been known as the go-to guy for non-traditional funeral work, whereas another shop we know well does great traditional designs. If you aren't known to the funeral homes in your area, it's time you changed that, and fast. Funeral directors will advise families as to where they can get flowers and will not recommend or suggest anyone they either don't trust or know.

As those florist experts, we need to build trust and relationships with those in the funeral business. You can begin to do so by finding out what their tastes and preferences are, so you can better serve their needs. These people are unique like all of us, and, like some, have certain needs and wants. (How's that for being "PC") I know of one place that *hates* flowers in vases, as they don't look like a "funeral." (Really?) Another who insisted that all water be poured out of any container so it wouldn't ruin their floors, and another who had a staff member who was allergic to lilies, so please don't send any! (Drugs are your friend, dear.) My old gay nerves, people! The folks who are paying should maybe have a say sometimes, don't you think?

Have you ever thought of sending out a permanent arrangement for the funeral home in your area? This can be a great way to build a relationship, as they will have this piece sitting in the showroom where they sell caskets and urns. (Is it called a showroom in a funeral home?) And it will serve as a beautiful reminder of your shop. Don't use cheap leftovers either, as a permanent piece is sometimes the first impression a family gets of your shop. (This holds true for fresh design work we send out as well.) I hate to hear florists say they send out their old flowers for funerals as they don't have to last anyway. Nice. Open flowers don't always mean old flowers, and there are only two things worse (can't tell you what they are) than going to a funeral for a visitation and seeing flowers that have been dead longer than Uncle Harry lying there. Use the best flowers you can for funerals as this will be remembered — as will the dead flowers that go out. Good floral design and fresh flowers are always well received, and you never know where some of the flowers are going to be used afterward. Word of bad flowers spreads like pee in a pool, and you can (and will) lose business very quickly.

I don't want a lot of flowers at my funeral (I'm not going for a while!). But don't think you're getting off easy! I want everyone who knows me to send flowers to someone they love that day, whether it's in Ireland or Inuvik. Flowers are a celebration of life — from the womb to the tomb — and we all need to celebrate!

25. Cherish the Moment

There are many "special" times in our lives that are to be celebrated, enjoyed, and remembered: first words or steps, perhaps your wedding (or divorce) day, the moment you finally ate a Krispy Kreme doughnut, or the first time you got to second base. You know, the standards. I don't know where a prom or graduation falls into the list for you, but prom especially was not a turning point in my life! (Oh my, I'm actually sitting here shuddering as I think of that night. I'd need a *Men in Black* "neuralyzer" to erase that one!)

Graduation is an important part of a person's life, for sure. It's also a time when we florists can help families celebrate the achievements of their wonder-child! I remember, years ago, working in a shop that did graduation bouquets for all the students; hundreds and hundreds of yellow roses were de-thorned, picked and tied for all to enjoy. Sadly, we aren't seeing as much of this sort of thing anymore, but it doesn't mean we can't evolve into doing other sorts of floral tributes.

More and more we are seeing graduations as a good reason to gather the clans and have a hoedown, so why not have flowers? Many plan a lovely night out or a family dinner at home before the graduate heads off to "find themselves" in Europe or to start work at the corner store. As many of you who know me might expect, I have no problem gently suggesting the use of flowers for a graduation party. Some of us get to decorate the stages for graduations, which is wonderful. Although many institutions feel their budget doesn't allow for it, the flowers really make for a difference.

Think of calling the graduation committee, student council, principal or whoever, and see about striking up a deal to do an arrangement for the stage, maybe in front of the podium for all to see? (Even permanent botanical flowers may suit.) This can be a great bit of advertising and allows you to really show off your talents to a targeted audience. As an exchange, you can offer discount or promotional cards for the grads, with offers for corsages, party centrepieces, or thank you arrangements for the parents.

Show an interest in the event and the customer's preferences, and you'll gain their trust. Really, this is what all of us want and need from our customers, and doing the *perfect* thing for this "most important day of their lives," at least as it's regarded in the moment, can lead to a lifetime of loyalty. I know this first-hand.

26. How to Work with Interior Designers

It seems like everyone's an expert these days, and it's getting harder and harder for us in our industry to keep our credibility, as well as to let everyone know that we are *so* much better doing floral design than they are! When a person comes in our store and says, "I do crafts at home!" (We all get those people, don't we?), I usually respond, "Well, what are you doing here then? Go home!"

There are those, however, who are very good at what they do, and we need to establish a relationship with them so we all can survive and grow.

I work with great cake people, photographers, wedding and party planners as well as interior designers and decorators. It has taken a lot of hard work and determination to build these relationships, and now I work with them all very well, rather than working for or under them. You know that feeling you get from some of them: you are "just the florist." That isn't a good fit on any of us, and we sometimes portray that very attitude ourselves, which is even worse!

Interior design and home décor folks are a great bunch to work with; it just takes a time to crack that nut. But believe me, it's worth it! I remember when I first started working with one designer in particular; I thought she was so mean and very impatient with me. I smiled (gritted my teeth), and did what

I needed to for her. After a time, she softened to the idea of actually asking me for an opinion, and then we started to become friends. I get it: they have an idea of what they want to create and often a floral piece is a make or break element in the whole look. The thing is to play nice and get along, just like Mum used to say.

There are many ways to get an "in" with interior designers, home stagers, and decorators. Every town, village, and city has some sort of home tour for a charity, so get your foot in the door by offering your work to them. I did this when we first started our store; the results were fantastic. Check out your local real estate agent and see if they use a stager for open houses, again offering your services. It seems as if everyone is having a home lottery these days too, so get your work in there, as there are lots of folks rooting through those homes, wanting to know who did what. Oh and here's a thought, *call* a few designers in your area. Chances are they don't know you, or much about you, so this is a great opportunity to let them know you are there to help. Send a sample of your work to them, remembering what trends are on the go, as well as (hopefully) knowing what their style is. Consider sending a lovely vase with a big monstera leaf and a branch in it, a dressed-up potted orchid, or a low cluster of roses (anything but red!), along with a note inviting them to your store to see the great décor products and ideas you have. This does cost a little money, and I can hear some of you cringe at the thought of sending out yet another freebie. Suck it up, sister; put on your big girl panties and deal with it! This is a guerrilla type of marketing and one that is much more effective these days than most others.

Trends come and go, and we have to keep on top of what's hot and new so we can stay current. If we do the same thing all the time and don't try to evolve, then we become stagnant and folks will see that. I did a design show for the folks at the Flower Group in Calgary, and they brought in some fantastic succulents for me to use. Well, there was a florist in the audience (who worked with an interior designer), who looked as nervous as a hooker in church. Turned out, she was just excited! She asked at the break if she could bring in her designer to see them (*of course* she could!), and they bought the lot of them.

It doesn't matter who it is, people assume you don't/can't do or provide the product or services they want if they don't see it on display. We get that a lot at this end of the country, as we are not the centre of the universe down here. So when a Great-I-Am comes in, I relish their look of shock and surprise when they see what we actually have.

Don't be afraid of the interior designers. In the scheme of services, they are merely the help, just like you and me, and when we work together we can make for a great finished project. Just be in the know by reading a shelter magazine or by watching "almost" any home décor show. (There's one on CBC, which shall remain nameless here, that makes me gag.)

27. Till Death and Beyond

I don't know if it's because I'm getting a little older (watch it!), or it's just nosy to see who's dropped this week, but I'm finding myself having a look at the obits in the papers now more than ever. I read about how wonderful the lives were of those now gone, what they've left behind, and the families and friends who carry on. Now, although there is a bit of a macabre feeling to all this voyeurism into deceased people's lives, I find it all genuinely interesting. As florists, we need (or should try) to know a little something about a person when we are creating a piece for them, especially if it's the last floral send-off for them. Reading the tributes is a great and accessible way for us to learn a bit and to be better prepared when orders come in.

I was a judge at a floral competition recently in the USA, where the competitors had to create a design by taking an obituary and interpreting it with flowers and other materials. I was impressed at the way these designers had to think and use their skills to create custom pieces to suit the obituaries. Many were so different; some had plastic fish, a stuffed dog, nails and screws, a hammer, a rolling pin and bowl, and even a big basket of Italian-themed foods incorporated into their arrangements. Strangely, the one piece I remember from this competition the most was the only one that didn't have one darned thing in it that made it different from any other arrangement. It was a lovely piece, well-made and very pretty, there was just nothing that made it unique. Really, it could have been used for a funeral, a birth, or a birthday. It was that generic.

These days, more than ever, we have to do what we can to attract, and retain, business through our doors. Let's face it, folks, funerals offer a great way to showcase what we can do. The last time I went to a funeral the place was covered in carnations, except for the one little thingy I did with a couple of callas and a big leaf. (I knew the lady liked callas.) I heard so many people comment on this one little design, and I received many positive responses from it. I've done pieces in the past using everything from an old pair of boots, a baseball and bat, and even a silk chiffon hat. (Yes, I did try it on!) You never know when someone is paying attention to your creativity, (or lack of it) so be aware that what you do today can help you out in the future. For example, I booked a rather large wedding last autumn because of a funeral arrangement I did for a family more than ten years ago. Apparently, I captured the spirit of the fellow, and they knew I was paying attention to their needs.

Funerals, for a lot of people, are like one big flower show (everyone's having a good look at all the arrangements), so here's where we can really showcase our work for a mass at a Mass! (Bad joke, I know!) Plants, glassware, and other non-traditional materials are becoming the norm in design now, so the more we can offer these tasteful alternatives to our clients, the better appreciated by the bereaved and the more likely we may become the go-to florist for all occasions. It's about being remembered for beauty, service, quality, and design, so when the urge hits a person to buy flowers, you'll be the one thought of.

Thank goodness for companies like Smithers-Oasis, too, who are always showing and providing the latest tools and techniques for us to use. Now more than ever we have access to all sorts of new wires, forms, foams, and accessories that can make our lives a lot easier, creative, and thus profitable. Even with the most traditional florists, there is always a place to add a bit of flair with a cool wire application or a frame, for example. Wrapping the pot of a plant with sisal or caging, or veiling an arrangement with bullion or angel hair can take your work (and reputation!) to another level very quickly and very cost-effectively. Check out your local wholesalers as they are great resources for new products and information.

Here's the key thing to remember about a funeral: talk to your clients! My goodness, we're so fast to get the order that we don't often stop to find out *who* the flowers are for instead of just *what* they are for. Find out what their lost loved one was interested in, if they were a gardener, a cook, a reader, etc. (And be sure you know the gender! I had an incoming order for a funeral, and the sending florist couldn't tell me if it was for a man or a woman!) For goodness sake, read the obituary if you get an order (you can do it online), and maybe you can get a heads up on what to offer the family.

There's nothing better than a good send-off, and it's up to us to make sure this happens. I mean, really, a funeral is a celebration of life, and flowers *always* celebrate life, so we're halfway there before we start! And (I *knew* one day I could use all these sayings) life goes on. So look to the future when creating the last arrangement for Uncle Henry, or whoever it may be. It could be the start of an enduring relationship!

28. Not That Old Thing Again!

When I first started in the floral industry, I was fortunate to be mentored, tortured, and trained by a master floral designer. (I also had feathered hair and platform shoes.) She showed me not only the most up-to-date styles and methods of design, but also spent time explaining how things were done years ago. I learned stuffing dirty wet moss in wreath frames, using dagger fern, chicken wire, or vermiculite to fill a vase, and how clay was used to secure flowers.

We live in a time of constant change, and yet we still go back to the old ways, don't we? (I actually saw someone wearing leg warmers. And no, I never wore them!) Wire is now "contemporary" and putting moss and/or soft clay in a design is more a decorative addition rather than a mechanic. I love seeing a newbie gleefully explaining their new-found discovery, when it's something us more "mature" designers have done for centuries! Remember "feathering" carnations or making a glamellia? I saw what we called a "Duchess Rose" being shown by a young designer who called it "a modern composite flower suitable for today's contemporary bride." Gotta tell you, I threw up a little on that one.

I was talking to my friend, the late Fred Caillie one day. Fred was a wonderful floral designer in our industry for a long (*long*) time. Anyway, he was saying how we've hurt ourselves with our evolution, and I totally agreed with him. I've been saying this for years, as the Martha wannabes have been creeping up around us with all their DIY projects. So many places that don't sell flowers or have a florist on staff offer fresh pieces for events, and not always very well done ones at that, and that makes us all look bad.

Fred suggested that we go out and get ten people off the street, give them all the same vase, and each the same bouquet of flowers. More than likely, seven of them will do an all right job. Then give the same group a dish with fresh foam and flowers. Betcha there won't be three that will do a job worth looking at. Doesn't that get you thinking?

Fresh flower foam was only invented in the 50s, and it revolutionized our industry. Since the birth of fresh foam, we've been able to design creative pieces in new and modern ways. What's more, the labour was cut significantly with weddings where so much had to be wired. Following this invention came new adhesives, containers, and other tools and accessories, all glorious things to make our lives better.

I watched throughout the 80s and into the 90s how bridal bouquets went from full and cascading in foam holders to increasingly simpler hand-tied clusters (clumps). Gosh, it got to the point that all one needed to do was grab a handful of roses and wrap them with an elastic band. (I actually saw that when a bride came in to get her bouquet fixed on her wedding day!) For those of us who aren't "I just do this for friends between trips to the bingo" people, it's kinda hard to justify any amount of labour charge for this sort of bouquet, isn't it?

I know, vase arrangements are less labour-intensive, cheaper to do, and faster to produce for many in our industry. They often are so generic that even the flowers look bored. I'm thrilled when I see a creative vase arrangement instead of another "seasonal mix" of flowers all plopped in a vase going in every direction, as it looks like a floral design and not like committee work gone wrong. (I just gave myself a headache.)

Thanks goodness floral foam is making a comeback. Fresh floral foam is our friend and when properly used will help us climb back to the top of the designer pile once again. Let's face it, you know as well as I do that the most talked about pieces you've ever done you've probably made in foam. Sadly though, so many of us have either forgotten how, or have never learned how, to properly use fresh foam.

Well, first, let it absorb water on its own. Don't hold it under water like you're drowning an old lover! Use fresh water with floral food dissolved in it. Keep the foam well-watered! Don't push and pull out stems from the foam, just one insertion per stem. Keep at your staff and co-workers so they know and remember these key points.

Oh my, I just went on like an old hen! Look it up, learn, refresh your memory, or upgrade your skills. Some of us are still not keen on using foam, fearing flowers don't accept food and water as readily in foam as they do in water. Well, the new Maxlife foam from Oasis is the cure for that, as it allows us to use flowers in foam that we've been afraid to in the past. (I did tests on my own, and believe me, it is pretty incredible!) Flowers like hydrangea, roses, and gerberas did very well in this new foam.

It's hard to keep up with what's in or out, what's new and what's crap, but we have to in order to keep up with everyone else. If you can Google (Ever Google yourself?) or flip a page in a florist's magazine, you can improve your skills. Don't be afraid to ask either. Lots of florists call, email, nag, drop in, or message me on Facebook looking for ideas or advice, and I'm thankful we can share our talents. It's up to us to improve and elevate floral design back to an art form in our communities. Now, go in peace, the Mass has ended.

29. Mind Your Own Business

What a wonderful life it is, owning a flower shop! We get to come to work when we feel like it; play with flowers, making pretty arrangements; and create beautiful displays for all to enjoy. How lovely our days are, filled with fun, laughter, and joy! *Wake up!*

What do you mean "balance the books"? They won't tip over! "Overhead?" What the hell is *that*? "I *must* still have money, I still have cheques left!" And what are these "margins" and "cost of goods" things I keep hearing about? This is a strange new language to those of us who start a business, at least for those of us who have never done so before. I got a terrible shock when I realized how little I actually knew about the business end of the floral business after signing a five-year lease! Boy, did I have my work cut out for me!

Ignorance isn't always bliss.

Thankfully, when we started this business, a business partner of mine did know some of the business aspects of running a store. Now, it was up to me to learn as much as I could as quickly as possible so I could run and understand my business. Thankfully, I had years of experience working in the industry and understood the value of time as well as the cost of each flower as it snaps off and hits the floor. Still, when it's your own shop you get a much clearer sense for sure!

I've owned this shop for over twenty-five years and still get arsed up when it comes to the business side of things. I do have a remedy, a saviour, a gatekeeper, a "no you can't" person who looks after so many painful things for me. We have someone who does our books, deposits, payroll, billings, and all the other nasty stuff that has to be done here at the shop, and I suggest hiring someone if you can afford it! (Think of the value of your time.) Now, don't think that I couldn't do all this if I *had* to; I just know that she can do it 187 times better and faster than me, which makes it very cost-effective. It's a luxury to know that I can stuff all pending paperwork in the drawer for someone else to look after. Then there's also another pair of eyes looking out for the business, which is important these days for sure.

Remember the days, boys, when "shrinkage" meant no more than a cold swim in the lake? Ah, good memories! In the flower shop it is just as upsetting, let me tell you!

Having your own store means that everyone who works with you should also learn at least some of what it takes to run a business smoothly. Take the snapped-off rose on the floor, for example. I get everyone to understand the cost of every flower and leaf being tossed, the cost of the sales slips they write on, the pens (well, maybe not the pens…they're usually hotel pens I collected on travels), etc. so they can get a better understanding of why things are how they are. In as much as it is important to teach your staff how to wrap a flower, talk on the phone, and clean the fridges, it is also imperative to teach them the value of the store and the importance of proper administrative work.

Some of the biggest challenges I have faced in this business involve paperwork: getting people to file things away properly, understanding sales slips and invoices, noting credits on invoices from suppliers, and finishing the cash sheets properly. It is shocking how much money you can lose because of simple errors or omissions. Look out when Ethel comes at me with an invoice flapping in her hand. That means someone messed up! And the old saying really holds true, "shit floats!" It doesn't matter who did (or didn't) do whatever it was they were supposed to do; it all floats up to you, the business owner, being responsible!

Years ago we got to do a rather large floral party for a group. We worked long into the night and when all was said and done, the party was a total success! We laughed and chatted about it for months. Here's the thing, we weren't the only ones laughing. No one took the time to prepare a bill and put it on the client's credit card. It was not a pretty scene here when Big 'n Bald found out, that's for sure! That's why now we check every sales slip at the end of the day to see that things are rung in and are looked after.

When I started My Mother's Bloomers back in 1992, I had pretty much a full head of hair, and I weighed fifty pounds less. Owning a flower shop is without a doubt one of the best things I have ever done, and for the most part

I have loved every minute of it! If I did have a little advice for anyone out there thinking of starting their own shop, it would be to arm yourself with as much knowledge as possible: read every floral publication, and learn from others whenever possible. I have had many call me for ideas, advice, etc., and I welcome it! We all need to work together in our industry in order to keep it alive and well.

I think I'll go play with my petals now. Have fun!

30. It Ain't Easy Being Green

Boy, Kermit the Frog sure said a mouthful when he sang that little song on the lily pad so many years ago. And here we are today, trying to do whatever we can to be, go, or become green! In our industry, there are many of us who have lived long enough to know the importance of the three Rs (reduce, reuse, and recycle) and have always practised them. I spoke to my friend Barbara Henzell (a master designer from Europe) in Toronto in January, and we joked about what we had to use and reuse in our industry years ago. This "trend" to go green is a mystery to a few, a revelation to many, and not more than a pain in the ass to others. I know how you feel, as we've all had thoughts run through our heads when we get the "environmentally conscious client" coming in wanting everything "bio-this" and "organic-that," dripping in diamonds and fur, yet not really understanding the whole picture. Going green can, however, be a great money-making opportunity too, and these days we've got to do what we can to get where we want to be!

My mother always said, "Waste not, want not!" as she cleaned and saved all the trays, tins, and tubs from the grocery store. (My brother tosses them in the blue bag as soon as she turns her back now!) I remember an old lady from my town that used to make a cup of tea and then hang the bag to dry! Now *that's* recycling! (Cheap old crow!) I find now, rather than saving everything in our flower shop, we're opting not to have it to start with whenever possible. It's amazing what we can do without, isn't it, when we put our minds to it? We're seeing packaging being less important (although I still love to see things wrapped and presented nicely), and when sending flowers out, we, in my store, are using biodegradable plastic when plastic is necessary.

Reusable containers for designing are what we use mostly here at our store. We don't use a third of those little plastic dishes (we used to call them PB100s) now, opting for ceramic, wicker, or glass instead. I know some of you are saying this isn't cost-effective, but these days a lot of these are cheaper than plastic. (Have you seen the flyers from your suppliers lately?) As for cost, a container that can be reused adds dollar value to a design, which is always a plus. Glass and ceramic add weight also which, unlike the weight that's resting on my arse-end, adds perceived value to a design. I had a conversation (well, she was a bit bitchy actually) with a "florist" about using glass and her need to use floral foam in everything. I love using floral foam and know how much of a help it is for designing. I'm not saying to stop using floral foam, but please, think to use coloured foam or simply wrap a leaf or ribbon around the foam before placing it in the vase for a decorative touch, or maybe learn a bit more!

Although we sell affordable luxuries in the floral and plant industry, we have to be careful as business people when making choices with our fresh purchases. Here at my store we are always asking where our flowers come from, knowing our suppliers are buying from socially and environmentally responsible farms whenever possible. Also, getting flowers trucked in rather than flown makes less of an impact on the environment, and using local suppliers is also beneficial to all. (There are some great growers here in Canada.) Here's the thing though, as a business, it's all well and good to do all these lovely things, and if it helps you sleep at night, good for you. It won't bring you any more business though, unless you tell your customers you're doing it. So in our store, we have a sign posted that describes just what we are doing. (I've received a lot of business from this one sign!) Many of us sell plants, which are a natural green addition to the home or office, and we need to promote their virtues from cleaning the air to calming stress. Some call this type of promotion "green-washing" which has a negative tone to it. I call it telling the truth!

For some time now we've been saving the sticks, leaves, and stems that otherwise would get tossed, and I take them home to compost them in my garden. I usually pile the bags up in the back garden all winter to use in the spring. It's amazing how much there is! (It's also amazing how many design knives and clippers I find too!) From this free gift of leftovers, I've been able to grow many of the summer flowers that we sell here at the store.

Folks are really getting into the swing of things now, thank goodness, and we're seeing not only water tubes being returned (gee, thanks!) but all sorts of glassware and other goodies, and we usually offer a few stems as thanks, which is so appreciated. This is a sort of recycling program, and although we don't openly promote it here (which wouldn't be a bad idea) many clients bring back their reusables.

Well, old Kermit, it really ain't that hard being green, just as long as you know what you're doing. Now, let's all sing (except you, Derrek in Winnipeg!) to the world of all the green things we do in our industry!

31. R U Upgraded?

I've seen a lot of new technology in the few years I've been an adult (ha!), and it's hard to keep up with, but as business people, we have to. I've witnessed the birth of colour television, affordable microwave ovens, the CD player (8-tracks for that matter!), and cellphones that weren't in Maxwell Smart's shoe! I remember when we got our first computer at work, and how important we all felt. Now I feel funny when I don't have my smartphone and laptop within reach at all times! What a world, eh?

I know there are many of us who either don't use the internet to our advantage or even have a web page, so pay attention as I tell you of the aches, pains, fun, and tortures that I went through (and still go through!) as I travel along the cyber highway.

Over the years, I've had our website changed so many times it made me crazy! (And you thought it was genetics that made my hair fall out!) The thing is to find someone out there who can set up a website who is knowledgeable, able to speak normal English and not just computer talk, and doesn't seem to cost an unreasonable amount. I have learned, the hard way, that this can take time, so research other sites in your local area, ask other florists who have set up their sites, and be sure to listen to what others tell you about what's worth and not worth having on a site. Call me! There are things I can't express clearly enough on any paper! Ha!

When we worked on the website we have now, there were things we wanted and didn't want on it (and others that we will change yet again). One thing we decided early on to leave out was those awful "intro" things that are on so many sites. We are in the "age of instant," and most skip all the fluff and music on a site. It's a waste of time and money for all involved! As a person who works a lot with the media, there is a phrase I always think of when advertising, online or wherever, "Information tells, while emotion *sells*!" So remember this for your sites. Flowers are a wonderful source of emotion, and we must use this attribute to our advantage. Photos, on the other hand, are a great resource, and by using photos of your work rather than generic photos, you'll develop a more unique site.

I have also done a few "how-to" videos that I use a lot for promotional purposes, and they have been very helpful, especially for those out of the country who don't know me or my work. I have a link for them on not only my site, but also on my agent's site (Imagine, me with an agent!), where they can have a look. There are also some videos that I have posted on YouTube that are specifically about flowers in different places in the world, which I get good feedback from, cost nothing (I shoot them with my camera), and are another possible revenue source. Check them out by searching "Neville on the Level." See, it worked already!

Really, the goal for me, and hopefully for you also, is to get your name out there in as many places as possible and as often as possible, so whenever folks are on the hunt for flowers in your area, they automatically think of you. Our store name is all over the web with our work on charitable events, wedding sites, and blogs from clients. These have all proven to be great (again, free) promotional tools for us, as we all like to support those who support our favourite charities, and many read testimonials and blogs about their favourite florists(and not so favourites).

Email has, for my business, become a must-have, and I freak (Is that the term?) when it goes down. Every day there are inquires that come in about doing an arrangement, an event or a wedding (often from a person sitting at an office desk!). It's here where I can offer advice, suggest a call would be better, or direct them to a website...or therapy.

I don't know about the rest of you, but I use the internet to do a lot of my buying now. I get many emails, e-newsletters, and e-specials on products and services that I would otherwise lose out on if I waited for the mail version, and although there are a lot of useless things that arrive in my inbox, it only takes a click or two to get rid of them. Oh, and for those environmentally sensitive folks who we all deal with, let them know this is a much more responsible way to communicate since there is no paper. (Insert peace sign here!)

One last, but very important thing to mention about using the internet to our best advantage, spell "evrythng korectly"! How annoying it is to get an email with all sorts of grammatical and spelling errors! Now, I'm no English major, but for goodness sake, put an effort in it! People pass judgment on how intelligent a person is by the way they write. (Don't you say a word, Arman Patel, *not a word*!) It took forever for me to figure out that "LOL" meant "Laugh out Loud!" and not "Lots of Love"! I thought Duane from Staalduinen was making a pass…Oh well, a boy can dream!

C U next time!

32. Here Comes the Bride

Have you ever watched the television show, *Bridezillas*? I have tried several times but always feel like going through the screen at them, so I doubt this can be good for my health. There are a lot of programs on now that showcase all the things that can (and sometimes do) go wrong when planning a wedding, and although it makes for good television, it doesn't make for a clear image of what most brides and their weddings are like.

Then there's the marvellous invention, the *internet*! This is where future brides can go to see images of what they may like to have, different flower combinations and all that jazz. The only bad thing that I have to say about this endless resource is that without knowing the availability, cost, and durability of the flowers online, often a bride can have some misconceptions and can be set up for disappointment when I have to sit her down and tell her "no."

I have so much fun with the wedding folks I work with and truly can say that although there have been some challenges in the past, there has never been a problem so insurmountable that the wedding was ruined. No flower, or lack of, can ever stop a wedding, and that is something we all need to know. I do feel for the bride who has her heart set on, let's say, peonies in August, and I have to chat her out of them. But really, there are *so* many flowers that are beautiful! This is why I try to always sit and have a good ol' chat with each bride, so we can go over everything involved.

We live in a time where there are a lot of options, and we are very fortunate! As a designer, I can always go to plan B (or plan C) if necessary, as things can happen with the weather, flights, colour, etc. I remember once when flowers for a wedding arrived pretty much cooked from the heat on the plane. After taking the necessary medication, I made a few calls and had more shipped right away, and the bride and her party were happy and looked fabulous. (And were none the wiser!)

Another time, there was a crop failure in California that caused me to totally redesign a bouquet, a hurricane spelled doom to flowers for another, and a greenhouse burned to the ground, halting any chance of me getting the flowers inside for yet another. Stuff happens, and sometimes we just have to roll with it. (Now you know why I have no hair!)

As a wedding flower consultant, I like to go over with my clients all the things that are needed, or not, for their wedding. Some of the things we talk over include the style and colour of the dresses (including hers), the time, date, and location of the wedding ceremony and reception, and if she has favourite flowers and/or colours that she "needs" to have included in the bouquets. Also I like to find out if there are any allergies or other issues that I need to know about.

Then we have an in-depth talk about the flowers, and what will be best suited for her and her wedding. There are many factors to consider when planning flowers for a wedding, like seasonal availability, themes, and location, all of which can determine the types of flowers chosen.

There are specific flowers that are very popular for weddings now, and will be for years to come, and I'll tell you of some of the flowers I love to use and why.

Roses have always been, and always will be, the most thought of flower for weddings. These regal blooms date to the first recorded weddings, and are known for their romance and beauty around the world. There are hundreds of varieties grown, and two of my favourites are Vendela (a soft cream standard) and Princess (small sprays of white flowers). I also fell in love with a newer variety of rose called Rosita Vendela, which has a lovely pink cast to the petals, as well as a green rose called Green Planet, which tends to keep its colour better than other green roses like Jade. Really, like I said, there are so many to choose from, and I am never at a loss for a beautiful rose for a bouquet.

Calla lilies are simply beautiful and beautifully simple. The single furl of the lone petal has a sexy charm to it, yet has a regal grace as well. The larger flowers are native to Africa and Australia, where they grow wild in the ditches, and are commonly called Pig Lilies! (How romantic!) I love to use the very popular miniature callas for wedding bouquets, clustering them on their own, or adding them with other flowers and greenery. They come in a good range of colours from whites and creams to pink shades, purple, yellow, and mango, and not only look great in a bouquet, but are known to last very well. I bring these little treasures in from Central America, where they are field-grown on the moist temperate hills year-round.

I am using a lot of hydrangea flowers for weddings again, which are grown in Central America. These can be a little fussy though, and need special care to ensure they will perform well.

Other than the ones mentioned, I must also include freesia, bouvardia, gerbera daisies, hypericum berries, and orchid varieties as other picks for bouquets.

I've been able to do a lot of fun floral things across Canada, and two of the latest included being part of a design team showcasing bridal work in the past hundred years and a design show in Toronto featuring weddings from across Canada. I also get the inside scoop on trends and the latest must-haves in our industry, so here's the scoop!

Clustering bouquets (you know, like the ones that "Stewart lady" was doing) were and still are very "in," and they will be for a time. We are seeing more types of flowers added to the mix though, whereas before there was often only one flower used. Also, the bouquets are having greenery added to "collar" the bouquet, and we are making the bouquets less structured, creating a softer and more romantic look.

Another trend in wedding work is the return to adding "bling" to bridal bouquets. Years ago it wasn't uncommon to have a bride bring in her mother's pearls or Grammy's brooch to include in her bouquet, and now there are glitzy stones, glass beads, coloured wire, and all sorts of neat things that can be added to a bouquet to give sparkle and shine. I do want to say that a little can go a long way with all this bling stuff. Remember that the most important things are the flowers, and the jewels must remain a subordinate. The worst thing to do is to have the "accent" fighting for attention with the focus of the design. Think of wearing a good pair of earrings, knowing that they are merely an accent to the whole picture, and not the main event!

Well, there are some of my thoughts about wedding flowers, and all the good, bad, pretty, and ugly that can happen. Weddings are beautiful, celebrating life and love. Although weddings aren't for everyone (while others like them so much, they get married again and again!), they remain one of the most important social and intimate events in a person's life.

This will be another year filled with the ringing of wedding bells, and I look forward to all the joys they bring! Nova Scotia is truly one of the *best* places for a wedding, with our scenery, world-class venues, and also all our beautiful people! Oh and in case you were wondering, David and I are married. And we are very happy this way!

All the best for a wonderful summer in Nova Scotia!

33. Are You Ready for Your Close-Up?

I remember the first time I was on a television show as a florist. I'd been on TV before that, but just as an audience member. I forget what exactly I was on for, because I was *so* nervous! I didn't sleep for days before the show, which was live, and I had to sit down because I was shaking so much. (This is not an attractive stance on a busty, larger man.) Anyway, I muddled my way through this nightmare and managed not to cut off my finger during my demonstration. Afterwards, as I was running for my life out the door, the producer said, "That was great! Wanna come back next month?" I replied, "Sure! Great!" What was I thinking? Anyway, I went back, and did spots on several shows, finally getting a biweekly gig on CTV Atlantic's (now) *Morning Live*, which I've been on for more than twenty years.

I got this first appearance — and, really, all my gigs — because of several factors. So pay attention and maybe you will be powdering your nose and stepping in front of the cameras sooner than you thought!

Be the expert they are looking for. Look, I don't know everything, as those who know me can easily attest, but what I do know I am willing to share with others. We are oral experts, but if the world doesn't know it, then we are wasting a valuable opportunity.

I remember a fellow from the newspaper who called about a spread he was working on for Mother's Day. He said they were doing stories on gift ideas and asked if I would like to place an ad. Well, I changed the direction from him trying to sell me an ad to *me* selling him on the idea of running a spread on fresh flowers! He could have a story, I told him, and in fact, I'd write it for free. He should just send a photographer over to get a few shots. It worked, and I was on my way to becoming a known oral expert.

Being an expert doesn't mean being a know-it-all, so don't be one of those cocky show-offs that make us want to change the channel. Look at the cooking shows and think of your favourite hosts; they are down to earth, knowledgeable, talk *to* you and not *at* you, sharing their knowledge and skills freely. I worked on a show once with a Great-I-Am who told me how stupid the audience was, that he would *never* speak with them, and that they were darned lucky, as was I, to have him in their presence. I was so offended, I wanted to release bees when he was on stage. It was a good lesson for me as a newbie though, because I knew I never wanted to be that bitter, old, ugly (I mean, uptight) person.

Selling the beauty of flowers is very important, so sell the aesthetic! Don't worry about getting too technical on TV, but make sure you're doing things correctly. I could go through the TV when I see someone making a mess of things because they don't know what they're doing.

I design with the audience in mind, so when doing a presentation for florists or a consumer show, I adjust the level of design, and how it's explained, to suit. Making yourself accessible is imperative, as no one wants to be looked down on, or made to feel stupid. I make fun of myself and my mistakes, and know that I am no better than anyone else; I just know different things. Remember also that a story sells, while information merely tells. Jazz up a "how-to" segment by sharing tales of how viewers can use what they're making, where the flowers come from, and so forth. It makes for more interesting viewing.

Things happen, especially when you're live on TV or on stage, so own it, and roll with it! I've had a vase break on TV more than once and have called a flower by the wrong name. In those instances, I calmly said, "Sorry, I'm just learning myself!" Once, I was interviewing a British fellow on stage in front of seven hundred folks when he dropped a bad (really bad!) word. I dealt with that as I do with most awkward situations. I laughed and said that was a no-no, and then we all laughed. I remember being on TV when another guest made lobster "shooters" and of course I had to try one. It was awful, and I stood there with a stupid smile, waiting for the shot to end so I could vomit. Only once I ran off camera screaming. We were doing a segment on the waterfront and a "friend" dropped by for a visit. It was a big ol' wasp that landed on the bouquet I was finishing. I had to get away but was so thankful that I didn't swear, or we would have made the six o'clock news!

Remember that folks want to see pretty flowers arranged beautifully, so show what you know. What you're doing is inspiring people with great design. They can't wait to try to do it themselves, and even if they can't do it themselves, it sure is nice to watch an expert in action. And they'll know who to call when they need their flowers done right!

About Neville

Neville, along with his husband David, owns and operates his cutting-edge floral shop, My Mother's Bloomers (since 1992).

His design talents have led to creating floral works for many celebrities and heads of state, including Sir Elton John, Sir Paul McCartney, Celine Dion, and members of the British Royal Family.

Neville is a member of the Canadian Academy of Floral Art, a community of florists in Canada and beyond who have reached the highest level of artistic achievement. Neville is also a member of Professional Floral Communicators - International, an elite group of international florists who have worked to achieve this designation as the go-to floral speakers throughout the world.

Neville is on the design and education team with Smithers-Oasis (North America), travelling worldwide to speak, present, and educate florists everywhere. Neville is a certified floral judge through the World Flower Council and is also a member of this international organization, dedicated to promoting flowers for World Peace.

Neville writes for Canada's premier floral trade magazine *Canadian Florist* and also contributes to many international publications where his work is enjoyed throughout the industry.

As an international speaker, you can find info on booking him at Vox Management Agency or www.voxagency.ca.

Neville has been on many television and radio programs, most notably more than twenty years as a biweekly guest on CTV Atlantic's *Morning Live* program. He has appeared on other television programs, including those on CBC Television, HGTV, and other national and international programs. Neville has been sought after by many for his quick wit, extensive knowledge of florals and plants, and his reputation as a public speaker.

Neville's philanthropy work is quite extensive, from hosting various fundraisers to providing flowers for others. He has received many awards, including a commendation from the Nova Scotia Lieutenant-Governor. Neville is a well-known presence on social media as well, and you can check out any photos, postings, blogs, and videos on his personal or business social media pages and websites.